Beyond ADD

Hunting for Reasons in the Past & Present

Beyond ADD

Hunting for Reasons in the Past & Present

by Thom Hartmann

Underwood Books
Grass Valley, California
1996

Beyond ADD
ISBN 1-887424-12-1 (trade paper)
ISBN 1-887424-13-X (hardcover)

Copyright © 1996 by Mythical Intelligence, Inc.
Distributed by Publishers Group West
Manufactured in the United States of America
Cover design by Nora Wertz/Nora Wertz Design
FIRST EDITION
10 9 8 7 6 5 4 3 2 1

The ideas in this book are based on the authors' personal experience with ADD, and as such are not to be considered medical advice. This book is not intended as a substitute for psychotherapy or the medical treatment of Attention-deficit Hyperactivity Disorder and the various medications described herein can only be prescribed by a physician. The reader should consult a qualified health care professional in matters relating to health and particularly with respect to any symptoms which may require diagnosis or medical attention.

Library of Congress Cataloging-in-Publication-Data:
Hartmann, Thom, 1951-
Beyond ADD : hunting for reasons in the past and the present/
by Thom Hartmann
p. cm.
Includes bibliographical references and index.
ISBN 1-887424-13-X (hardcover). --ISBN 1-887424-12-1 (pbk.)
1. Attention deficit-hyperactivity disorder. I. Title.
RJ506.H9H383 1996
616.85'89--dc20   96-26376
                                                    CIP

"To have ADD is to have a lifetime of struggle."
— Overheard at an ADD conference

This book is dedicated to Gerhard and Gerda Lipfert of Höchheim, Germany: two pioneers who have changed the world, one person at a time.

"We measure ourselves by many standards. Our strength and our intelligence, our wealth and even our good luck, are things which warm our heart and make us feel ourselves a match for life. But deeper than all such things and able to suffice unto itself without them is the sense of the amount of effort we can put forth... He who can make none is but a shadow; he who can make much is a hero."
— William James

Acknowledgments

Special thanks go to Rob Kall for providing some inspirations and many quotes used in the chapter headers of this book. Thanks also to Carol LaRusso for her marvelous editing work on this and my previous four books on ADD. And to Tim Underwood, my publisher, for having the courage and persistence to advocate for our "different perception" of ADD.

Thanks to Drs. Marilyn Lalka and Beth Bradford for their input; to Pablo Villegas, MD, for the insights he shared when we were roommates in Beijing studying acupuncture; to Tom Allen, Karl Pribam, Michael Hutchison, and Siegfried Othmar for all they taught me about how the brain functions; to Jerry Schneiderman, Jack Rieley and J. for their encouragement; to Dick Gregory for his good humor when we were in Africa dodging bullets; to Elisa Davis, Janie Bowman, Carla Nelson, Susan Burgess and the staff and members of the ADD Forum on CompuServe who've helped me (and challenged me) as I worked through ideas; to Dave deBronkart whom I will always consider one of this planet's most gifted and extraordinary human beings; and to my mentor and teacher, Gottfried Müller, his family, helpers, and assistant; to John Ratey, Med Hallowell, Harvey Parker, and Raun Melmed for all they've taught me about the medical and psychological viewpoints of ADD, and their encouragement and friendship.

The most important acknowledgments, however, go to my wife and children who have taught me so much about ADD and about life, and to all the CHADD, ADDA, and other ADD support group and chapter leaders who have invited me to speak from coast to coast in the USA, Israel and Europe. Thanks!

Contents

Acknowledgements   viii

Introduction: **Why We Have ADD**   xiii

1. **ADD is Profitable for Business**   1

   ADD is Profitable   3
   Pop Psychology and the Media Encourage Victim-
   ness and Illness   7
   ADD is Viewed as "Bad" Because Only "Bad"
   People Have Been Studied   12

2. **Education and Our Children**   15

   "Good German Schools" Come to America   17
   American Schools Focus on Content Instead of
   Technique   25
   Our Gifted Kids are Bored Silly   28
   Education is More Important Today than in Years
   Past   34
   Visual Learners in Auditory Schools   38
   We Now See More ADD Because of Standardized
   Curriculum   42
   Our Children are Losing Empathy Abilities   46

3. **Genetics and Psychology**   51

   ADD Characteristics- Leftover Hunter Genes   53
   What Maslow Overlooked: The Need to Feel Alive   65
   ADD As Hypervigilance Run Amok   84

4. **Social Adaptations**   95

   ADD Prevents Human Society from Ossifying   97
   Morphic Resonance: The Hundredth Monkey
     Phenomenon   101
   "Normal" People Are Really "Abnormal"   107
   Our Culture is Increasingly Intolerant of "Dif-
     ferent" People   112
   The Perception of Time   116

5. **The Stress and Toxicity of Modern Life**   121

   Our Toxic Environment Neurologically Damages
     Fetuses   123
   Nutritional Deficiencies   126
   Ritalin is Such a Cool Drug   129
   Life in America (and the Rest of the Industrialized
     World) is Getting Crazy   133
   We're Living in the Last Days and the World's
     About to End   138
   There Are Too Many People   143

6. **Brain Chemistry and Physiology**   147

   Brain Irritations   149
   Sugar and Sugary Foods Alter Brain Chemistry   153
   Dysfunctional or Underdeveloped Frontal Brain
     Lobes   156
   ADD as a Variation of Normal Male Behavior   159
   ADD is Not Just One Thing   162
   Some "ADD" May Really Be Undiagnosed Thyroid
     Disorders   167

7. **Contemporary Lifestyles and Habits**   171

   Advertising "Causes" ADD by Training Us to Have
     a Short Attention Span   173
   A Variation on Approach/Withdrawal: Why ADD
     Often Appears Different in Women than in Men   180
   We Lack Self-Discipline-Inducing Experiences in
     Childhood   183
   Sunlight Starvation   186
   We Lack Exercise   189
   ADD is Useful in Our Workforce   192

Our Lost Rituals   196
ADD as a Challenge to Authoritarian Society   199

**Summary: What Is This Thing Called ADD
Anyway?**   203

Chapter Notes   205

About the Author   209

Index   211

Introduction: Why We Have ADD

A boy or young man who has some serious constructive purpose will endure voluntarily a great deal of boredom if he finds that it is necessary by the way. But constructive purposes do not easily form themselves in a boy's mind if he is living a life of distractions and dissipations, for in that case his thoughts will always be directed towards the next pleasure rather than towards the distant achievement. For all these reasons a generation that cannot endure boredom will be a generation of little men, of men unduly divorced from the slow process of nature, of men in whom every vital impulse slowly withers, as though they were cut flowers in a vase.
— Bertrand Russell, *The Conquest of Happiness*

Bill, 37, was diagnosed with ADD (Attention Deficit Disorder) three years ago and takes Ritalin daily. He's always been a whirlwind, flying from one thing to another his entire life. He's flown through three wives, dozens of extramarital affairs, 23 jobs, and four attempts to finish his first year of college. His IQ was once measured at 147, and another time at 121: he flew through the test the second time. Bill likes to think on his feet, so much so, in fact, that he's constantly pacing, and can't tolerate meetings where he has to sit for more than fifteen minutes at a time. He's gotten 14 traffic tickets in his life, all but one for speeding, and has been in three spectacular accidents, breaking a total of 11 bones. As a teenager he tried every drug that came by, and still enjoys cigarettes, coffee, and alcohol, although he insists that the only one of the three he's addicted to is nicotine.

Margie, 29, was diagnosed with ADD last year and also takes

Ritalin daily. She's an attractive woman who's been happily and faithfully married to the same man since she was 19. She has a degree in English and graduated cum laude, although she will tell you that to do that she had to work twice as hard as anybody else she knows. She had a study partner through much of college, and leaned heavily on her husband for academic support as well. Her IQ consistently tests around 126, although most of her friends would describe her as "a little bit dingy." She constantly forgets her car keys, her purse, directions to her destinations, and is always late for meetings or appointments. She's quiet, soft-spoken, and her home seems well-organized—until you look in the closets. Few people realize how smart she is, and many hardly even notice her because she so rarely speaks up or draws attention to herself. Many times she's learned, after the fact and to her dismay, that people thought she didn't like them or was judging them negatively because she was so withdrawn around them.

Kathy, 47, was diagnosed with ADD three years ago and takes Desoxyn daily. A registered nurse and the mother of four children ages 8 to 16, she's described by her friends and relatives as "the responsible one." Kathy can always be counted on to pitch in when things are tough, and her friends and relatives all know it. She's patient, methodical, and well- organized. She's outspoken, and everybody knows exactly where she stands on just about any issue. In the operating theater she is one of the best nurses in the city: totally focused on the job at hand, anticipating the doctor's needs, monitoring everything around her with a careful and practiced eye that rarely misses a thing. She can keep this pace up for hours at a time.

Bill, Margie, and Kathy are all very individual. If you were to line them up in a row and tell a stranger that they all shared an identical psychological disorder, that person would probably protest that you were wrong, that these three are as different as any three random folks off the street.

Yet all three have ADD, at least by our current definitions.

The definition of ADD is often a slippery thing. A dozen people with the same diagnosis each can seem very different in their behaviors, ranging from hyperactive to withdrawn, from forgetful to obsessively hyperfocused.

Because of this variability of the different aspects of ADD, some experts such as Dr. Lynn Weiss have theorized that several subtypes of the condition exist, each manifesting in different ways. This is no doubt true, and even the American Psychiatric Association's (APA's) DSM IV has now classified at least two subtypes of ADD; some experts theorize there may be as many as a dozen more.

This variability has also given skeptics ammunition to argue that any condition with such a wide range of symptoms can't be a real diagnostic category in and of itself. To quote Rush Limbaugh, "There is no such thing as ADD." After all, they point out, a schizophrenic is pretty obviously schizophrenic, as is a person who's manic, or severely depressed. Even the more recently defined and arguably gray-area conditions such as Post Traumatic Stress Disorder (PTSD) and Chronic Fatigue Syndrome (CFS) are rather clear when compared to the spectrum of behaviors various writers and diagnosticians have labeled as being facets of ADD.

ADD, however, either because it's a relatively new category or because it may actually represent a spectrum of subtypes or even different conditions, is a bit harder to nail down. There are those whose ADD is hyperactive and expressive: the classic problem-boy in school. And in those whose ADD is internalized, their days are filled with raging discussions in their own mind but few words ever escape their lips. The ADD of some people expresses itself as disorganization, whereas for others it's best observed in their tendency to hyperfocus when charged with stress but to be unfocused or impulsive in ordinary daily circumstances.

So what is this thing called ADD? Where did it come from?

In my earlier books on the topic I've put forth as a primary model the concept of Hunters and Farmers.

ADD, I argued, is something that was once an adaptive psychological and physiological mechanism providing our hunter/gatherer ancestors with an edge over the world in which they lived. Their distractibility was actually a continual scan for danger or opportunity in the world of the forest or jungle; their sense of doom was a hypervigilance that protected them from predators or enemy warriors; their impulsivity eliminated the problem of indecisiveness which could cause them to miss out on a meal if they were busy doing a task while something edible ran by; their seeking out of sensation and risk facilitated their hunt, leading them into areas where food could be found (along with the other predators also attracted by that food).

I originally proposed the Hunter/Farmer model of ADD merely as a paradigm, a story that children or adults could tell themselves about who they are and where they came from. This would be less disempowering than a medical model that says, "You're mentally disordered." Over the years since I first proposed it, however, a number of scientists have come forth with evidence that there may actually be some (perhaps even much) truth to the notion that ADD is a vestigial survival mechanism handed down to us from our ancestors.

But it's also not that simple.

We know, for example, that something very much like ADD can be caused by some types of illness. The earliest diagnostic category which we now call ADD was, in fact, a set of behaviors observed among children who had suffered from the brain infection of encephalitis. It was then called Minimal Brain Damage (MBD), later redefined as Minimal Brain Dysfunction as doctors noticed the symptoms among people who'd never had encephalitis. Then finally it was known as Attention Deficit Disorder and its current variations.

There's also the very real issue of whether a person with a mild case of ADD has a disorder at all: they may, in fact, be even more functional and successful in many arenas than their peers who don't have ADD. While severe ADD can lead to failure in many aspects of life, even here it may be what causes people like Thomas Edison or Evil Kneevil to be as successful as they are in particular and limited areas of their lives.

My first three books on ADD tried to define the symptoms of ADD, offered a reframing of it into something that could be useful in some context, and shared with people specific strategies for understanding, overcoming, or even using their ADD to good advantage.

This book is different in that it seeks to understand more deeply what this thing we call ADD is—to explore some ideas about where it came from, and why so many people today are being diagnosed and medicated for it.

You'll find here a spectrum of theories and ideas ranging from the medical to the metaphysical, from the common-sensical to the esoteric. All are concepts that have (in my opinion, at least) some merit—and none of them totally explain ADD. Yet each idea offers us a bit wider insight, a broader view, a deeper understanding into this condition which is increasingly becoming part of the average person's vocabulary.

Keep in mind as you read that I'm neither endorsing nor advocating any of these particular points of view: this book is intended as a platform for discussion. I continue to believe that the Hunter/Farmer model is probably the best and most accurate explanation for why we have ADD in our gene pool. I think it offers the most comprehensive insights into what we can do to help people with ADD succeed in work, school, and relationships, but even that is far from a certainty.

Nonetheless, each of these ideas bears consideration. The more insights we can gain into ADD and its relation to our lives, and work or school situations, the stronger a grip we can get on the lever of change in our lives.

It may well be that what we're calling ADD now will, in ten years, be broken into a dozen other, different categories, many having little or nothing to do with attention, deficits, or disorders. Some of the chapters in this book explain not what ADD is but why we're seeing it being diagnosed and treated so much. While they may seem synonymous, these different hooks into ADD represent a significant difference in point of view.

It's my hope that this book will stir debate and dialogue about what ADD is, where it came from, and why so many people are wearing the label. This is an important issue regardless of any individual position, and people advocating different points of view will probably find both ammunition and refutation in the pages that follow.

Thom Hartmann
Roswell, Georgia
January 1996

Beyond ADD

Hunting for Reasons in the Past & Present

CHAPTER ONE

ADD is Profitable for Business

Television and radio glorify frailty and illness through daytime talk-shows, convincing a nation of habituated "couch potatoes" that it's cool to be neurotic.

Our colleges and research institutions have little interest in studying what non-pharmaceutical kinds of healing actually work in people, because they're largely funded by pharmaceutical and food manufacturers. Little research is done on what makes people successful because there is little profit to be made in "helping" people who are already successful in taking care of themselves. The result is that we have only the vaguest notions about what works to make people healthy and successful, while we have tons of research on every aspect of weakness or illness.

Most bizarre of all, our "healthcare" industry only gets money when people become sick.

This opening chapter for *Beyond ADD* takes a look at all of these factors and considers how they may relate to the explosion of ADD and ADD diagnoses we're seeing in the industrialized world.

ADD is Profitable

"The business of America is business."
— Calvin Coolidge, 1872-1933

During the Christmas holidays in 1995 I visited a friend who's a healer of some note. He's worked with all manner of serious diseases, particularly cancer.

"We're getting better and better at screening for cancer," Don said. "Expect to see more and more things like the PSA (Prostatic Specific Antigen) blood test in the future, techniques that will indicate cancer in the body before there's a detectable tumor."

"Sounds like good news," I said.

"It's certainly good business," he said.

"Good business?"

"Yep. A cancer diagnosis is worth about $250,000 to the medical establishment."

"That sounds like a pretty cynical thing to say," I said. "You don't mean to say that doctors are looking for cancer because it makes them money?"

"Not individually," Don said, "although there are probably a few cynical exceptions. But what you have to understand is that we're part of a sickness industry, not a wellness industry. If people were well, there would be a heck of a lot of people out of work."

"You don't think that those people would be glad to be out of work if it meant fewer people dying?" I said.

Don shrugged. "If a jumbo jet with 300 people on it crashed once a week for six months, 26 jets going down in cities all over

America, over seven thousand people dead, what do you think would happen?"

"I'd sure not get on another plane," I said, laughing.

Don wasn't smiling. "Seriously."

"Well, there would be calls for congressional investigations, the FAA would be in a fit and if something wasn't done the commissioner of the Federal Aviation Administration (FAA) would be fired, the airlines would be working frantically to try to find out why all those planes were falling out of the sky, and nobody would fly."

"Be a pretty damn scary thing, right? Major national scandal?"

"Yeah."

"Ok," Don said, "let's imagine that every single day of the year *four or five* big jets went down. Yesterday there were crashes in New York, Chicago, San Diego, Denver, and Las Vegas. The day before that planes went down in Detroit, Cleveland, Miami, and Honolulu. The day before that planes had crashed in Portland, Seattle, Dallas, Phoenix, and Boston. And so on. Every day four or five planes full of people, and everybody died. Can you imagine the uproar?"

"The country would be hysterical," I said.

"That's the number of people who died today, yesterday, the day before, and every day this year just from smoking. Now, what's wrong with this picture?"

"There's no national hysteria."

"Right. Only one guy in all of Congress, Henry Waxman, even talks about this. They'll probably blow him out of the water in the next election. And while the AMA has given lip service to the issue, they only did that very late in the game. The medical establishment is one of the three most powerful lobbies in the world. Doctors are viewed as priests of the high religion of medicine: if we really started speaking out, loudly and strongly, we could outlaw tobacco in six months. But it's not going to happen, because nearly every one of those 450,000 people who die from cigarettes each year generate about a quarter-million dollars apiece for the medical establishment. That's $112,500,000,000 for the medical industry: we make more off smoking than the tobacco companies."

As I was driving to the airport from Don's house, his words ringing in my ears, I thought about the TV special that had tried to make ADD support groups look bad because some had accepted contributions or grants from CIBA, the manufacturer of Ritalin. I know many people in these support groups, including their founders and some of their board members. There is no doubt in my mind they're well-intentioned good people who are working hard to help children and adults with ADD. Most are the parents of ADD children themselves. And none, to the best of my knowledge, are profiting from ADD.

But such organizations have also sponsored national conferences where some members of the medical establishment—people who do make money from diagnosing and treating ADD, principally through prescribing drugs—have strongly advocated the use of drugs and ridiculed all theories and treatments without drugs at their core. I attended several speeches where sarcasm and ridicule were so strong and pointed, so cutting and accusatory, that I sat in slack-jawed amazement. Had I been the researcher who'd earlier presented the work on ADD and EEG Neurofeedback and who was the target of one of these attacks at a 1994 conference, I would have felt devastated.

Nonetheless, I don't believe that the physicians and psychologists who assert that ADD is an "illness" are doing so just to make money than I believe that the average general practitioner or oncologist wants people to start smoking. Yet all are part of an industry that profits from "illness."

Which comes back around to my friend Don's point—we have in this country a sickness-based health-care industry, rather than a wellness-based one. This is in contrast to ancient China, where you paid the doctor every month while you were well; when you became sick, you paid nothing until you were well again. Doctors of those days were proactive practitioners of preventative medicine.

So long as we define ADD as a sickness, it falls into the arena of a huge industry which earns hundreds of millions of dollars a year from the diagnosis and treatment of this condition. This which will always encourage more diagnoses and more treatments, even in those cases where it may not be ADD at all, or only in the most marginal sense.

Solutions

The best strategy to avoid becoming the victim of an industry seeking its own self-interest rather than yours is education. Don't just listen to one theory or party line, but get as much information, and as many dissenting views, as possible. Examine each one critically, and ask if there are hidden agendas at play which may have skewed the information to the benefit of the information provider.

This is good advice whether we're buying a new car, a house, a computer, a toy, or psychiatric/psychological/medical services. Be an informed consumer, and take nothing for granted.

Pop Psychology and the Media
Encourage Victimness and Illness

When the patient loves his disease, how unwilling he is to allow a remedy to be applied.
—Pierre Corneille, *Le Cid*

If you look through the index of the Diagnostic and Statistical Manual of Mental Disorders, often referred to as the DSM, published by the American Psychiatric Association, you will not find the word "normal" listed. This shouldn't come as a big surprise: the DSM is about psychiatric abnormalities, and the business of the psychiatric and psychological industries is to assist persons with problems.

However, it does point up one overarching reality that extends well beyond just the field of psychiatry: we have a culture which has become obsessed with illness while it often ignores or overlooks wellness.

This has lead to the labeling of many relatively "normal" parts of the human condition as pathologies. In the modern recovery movement, people are often encouraged not to become stronger or resilient but instead to wallow in their weaknesses and to search for villains at which to point the finger of blame. These villains range from parents, to pesticides, to "brain abnormalities" such as ADD.

But for many this is merely an easy out, a technique for shifting away personal responsibility. The idea that such "weaknesses" or "damage" will automatically cause us to fail is, in fact, not at all consistent with reality. For example, studies of "at risk" children done over the past 30 years (the most famous one being a study done in Hawaii) show that children from abusive, alcoholic, "broken" and poverty-struck homes are far more likely to grow up as healthy, well-adjusted adults than they are to grow up mentally ill, neurotic, or "damaged."

How could this be?

Two pioneers in this field, Drs. Stephen and Sybil Wolin, in their book *The Resilient Self*, posit what they call the "Challenge Model" of childhood development as the answer. In this view of human development, children use adversity as a tool to develop their own inner strengths and resiliences. While they often emerge into adulthood with scars (virtually everybody does), they also come through this difficult process of growing up with powerful strategies for dealing with adversity. In fact, these children are often far more successful and adaptive as adults than are the children of "normal" families.

Unfortunately, the Challenge Model is not known to most people, whereas the idea that people are damaged irreparably by their negative childhood experiences has so thoroughly infiltrated our popular media and the public's notions of psychology that it's considered an irrefutable truth.

This glorification of frailty has led us to both trivialize serious mental illnesses, and to view substantial parts of the what was once called "human nature" as neatly organized little disease categories. Wendy Kaminer in her book "I'm Defective, You're Defective," points this out with excruciating insight. She shows how an advertising-hungry media and a run-amok victimness movement have shifted our view from the appropriate analysis of human differences into an hysterical search for our own particular mental illnesses, weaknesses, or category of victim status.

The upshot of this is the explosion of fads, books, and recovery groups, and the apparent desire of just about every good citizen to figure out which particular mental illness they are suffering from. "You Americans astound me," Dr. Oswain Gierth of Germany told me a few months ago. "You spend so much time looking at and for behaviors and conditions that you can create labels and treatments for. Much of what you call ADD over there,

here in Germany we would just call part of the spectrum of human behavior."

It's reached the point where when I speak at ADD support groups, the majority of people who want to talk with me after my speech are anxious to proclaim their own ADD, as if it were a badge of honor to have a DSM-certified mental-illness label. While I'm proud that I'm a "Hunter" at heart, I would be reluctant to brag to anybody that I have a mental illness.

Much of this is fueled by the flood of books, magazine articles, and TV talk-shows which wallow and revel in emotional and mental pain, illness, and victimhood. Rarely do such media ever portray the wonders of resilience, or mention that over 70% of the children of severe alcoholics grow up with no alcohol problem, or tell us that the majority of people who suffered severe abuse as children are quite functional as adults, thank you very much.

By buying into the notion that a person is "damaged goods" because he or she had a painful childhood or is neurologically off the norm, we disempower that individual. We imply to them that they'll never be successful without our (often expensive) help, that they're lacking in inner resources, and that they're fundamentally flawed. This can cause a person to become locked into a lifelong cycle of victimness which, while obsessing on their weaknesses, never gives them an opportunity to develop or use their own internal strengths.

And yet, research shows clearly that it's often these very life-pains and neurological differences themselves which can be a *source of strength* when reframed and viewed in a positive light.

An article in *The Journal of Learning Disabilities* sought to identify those patterns of behavior or thought which had helped adults with learning disabilities to be successes instead of failures. The single most important variable, they found, was the degree to which the people viewed their disabilities in a positive light, rather than in a negative way. Those people who saw themselves as damaged goods were far less likely to be successful than equally-"disabled" adults who instead viewed their differences as unique creativities or eccentricities.

Similarly, in the Hawaii studies, it was found that those

children who viewed their abusers or painful life situations as adversities to overcome were most likely to be resilient and emotionally strong as adults. They often grew up successful and highly functional, in sharp contrast to their equally-abused or poverty-stricken peers who passively surrendered themselves to the situation and then, as adults, failed and blamed their failures on their past, on others, or on themselves.

Unfortunately, the majority of our media and spokespeople for the "helping professions" rarely encourage people to view their adversities and challenges in a positive light. Instead, there's a stampede on to join the victim-of-the-month club.

In this frantic search for victimness, the ADD label is a convenient one for many people. In many cases this is because whatever it is that we call ADD *really is a problem*. But in many other cases, it's the search for a scapegoat, an excuse, or even an excuse to identify with a group. In some circles it's now as "in" to have ADD as it was to have Chronic Fatigue Syndrome fifteen years ago.

And so, myth or not, seriously afflicted or not, many people are pinning the badge of ADD upon themselves and their children, swept up in the tide of this latest darling of pop psychology. Unfortunately, instead of looking for possible ways to work through or around ADD, many in the recovery movement (which the ADD support movement has sometimes morphed into) focus entirely on "brain abnormalities," "co-morbidities," and the latest medication.

Solutions

There are potential dangers for people with ADD in the recovery movement that's now springing up around this label. Most in it are well-intentioned, honest, and very helpful people: many lives are being improved and people saved from failure and disaster. But there are also shameless self-promoters with overpriced books and videotapes, or who organize "support groups" only to exercise personal power over others, or label others as sick only because they can then sell them a palliative (some even involving exposures to radiation or experimental drugs, in a fashion painfully reminiscent of the radium-treatments children were routinely given in the 1950's which led to an explosion of thyroid and other cancers in later life). And so the ADD movement grows, more are swept into it, and pretty soon the backlash will begin with people calling ADD a myth, a made-up category, and a non-disease.

Of course the backlash folks are as wrong as are the "half the population has ADD" promoters. The reasonable middle-ground is that there is such a thing—or things—as ADD/ADHD, but that much of the hysteria and hype surrounding it is misplaced or in-place only to serve special interests. We must seek a rational middle ground, acknowledge and nurture the often-considerable strengths to be found in ADD individuals, and help them bring these out and develop them as life skills. And we must be very careful of the fad-of-the-month syndrome, and those who would offer instant remedies or "for your own good" hand-holding.

Additionally, since TV and radio pop-psychology talk-shows often encourage the notion of "I'm a powerless victim" or "there's always an excuse," it may be a good idea to limit children's exposure to them. There's a growing trend in America to totally disconnect the TV altogether, and those families who have tried it invariably report that their children become more independent, read more, and interact with family and friends more.

ADD is Viewed as "Bad" Because Only "Bad" People Have Been Studied

That's all we may expect of man, this side
The grave: his good is—knowing he is bad.
  —Robert Browning, The Ring and the Book, 1868

I was sitting in the back of the auditorium as a psychologist and self-professed "ADD expert" lectured to a roomful of ADD adults. "Don't you people realize you're all sick?" he said, a tone of criticism in his voice. (He was following a speaker who'd just said there might be some good sides to ADD, a position with which he vehemently disagreed.) "You have a disorder!" His voice became shrill: "When I worked in the prison system, I saw hundreds of people like you! They're all ADD in there! This is a mental illness, dammit, and if you don't believe it let me take you into a jail for an afternoon!"

It was a thoroughly depressing speech. He gave the case histories of a compulsive rapist, a repeat burglar, a homeless man who'd died under an underpass, and two of his female patients currently in the mental hospital. One was now HIV positive either because of her drug abuse or her promiscuity. I could see shoulders drooping all over the room, heads hanging in shame and embarrassment, as this group of ADD adults were told in graphic detail how severe was the mental illness with which they were afflicted.

Later in the week, I recounted the story in part to Dr. Dale Hammerschmidt, a physician in Minnesota on the faculty of a medical school and the parent of an ADD child. His response on CompuServe's ADD Forum was so commonsense it startled me:

"When I was in medical school in the 1960s, we learned a lot about homosexuality and homosexuals. We learned about the nature of the homosexual relationship, the tendency to fleeting unions, the difficulty forming a durable attachment, the tendency to depression, the tendency to sexual aggression, and the often abnormal family dynamics.

"The problem was that the data were all gathered on the homosexuals who were available to be studied in the 1950s– almost exclusively ones who came to psychiatric attention because of problems related to their sexuality.

"So what we were really learning about, perhaps quite accurately, was a sub-set of homosexuals unhappy with their sexuality or those who had been convicted of (homo)sexual offenses. It was then quite common to generalize those data to all homosexuals.

"But that seems to have been way off the mark: now that the socially well-adjusted homosexuals are more open, we find that a lot of what was once thought to be true for all was true only for a small and unhappy fraction. This was particularly unfortunate, in that the earlier data, when uncritically extrapolated, gave grounds for defining homosexuality to be a mental illness, and lent support to all sorts of discrimination. The echoes are still being heard.

"It's an example I've thought about often, in part because that earlier research has often been described in disparaging, even condescending terms by people writing now. They never seem to ask why those earlier results were obtained; and if they do, they claim it was just flagrant, homophobic bias.

"But like most things in life, the truth is a bit more complicated. We had a long-standing societal bias against homosexuals; that led to the facile assumption that the patients available for study were representative. So there was a (non-deliberate) ascertainment bias– the results were probably correct, but for a much narrower population than was guessed. The 'homophobic' bias was subtle, just enough to make it take several years to address the should-have-been-obvious question: How sure are we that these results apply to *all* homosexuals, rather than just those we've been able to study?"

Likewise, what is the population that has been studied with regard to ADD/ADHD over the past thirty years? *It's been exclusively drawn from among children and adults who have failed or crashed in some way in their lives. They've ended up in special* education, in institutional settings, in jail, in mental hospitals, and in the offices of psychiatrists and psychologists.

I do not know of a single study which went out into the real world of "normal" people and tried to ascertain how many of them have ADD but succeeded anyway. The mental health institutions and drug companies which fund research are interested largely in helping (and selling help to) people in pain and in need, not in figuring out why normal people are normal or successful people are successful.

So it should come as no surprise that a psychologist who had worked with ADD prisoners would have a jaundiced view of the chances of an individual with ADD—the only people he'd ever seen with ADD were prisoners! Similarly, it shouldn't surprise us that most of the literature on ADD emphasizes pathology and illness, failure and consequence, rather than strength and success. The failing population was studied exclusively.

In the face of this observation, one could argue that the "normal" people weren't studied because they couldn't be ADD. By definition ADD is a "disorder," and somebody who's not suffering or failing isn't disordered. But the large and growing number of adults I see at ADD support group meetings and hear from on CompuServe don't describe themselves as disordered. They are not having major crises with their lives, and yet they are diagnosed and medicated for ADD.

The main reason ADD may be so strongly argued by so many people to be a "bad thing" is because only the failing population has been evaluated. As ADD moves more and more into the mainstream and the popular culture, we may see it viewed more as an attentional "difference" than a "disorder."

Solutions

ADD is constantly being redefined. It wouldn't surprise many ADD experts to see a less severe diagnostic category emerge in the next few years to describe people with moderate levels of distractibility, impulsivity, and sensation-seeking. This category probably wouldn't contain the word "disorder," but would instead be described as a syndrome or personality type.

CHAPTER TWO

Education and Our Children

Give the average American teenager a computer—a box containing a Pentium processor, color monitor and card, keyboard, mouse, modem, and four software programs—and within a week he or she will have figured out how to find just about anything on the Internet, and probably even will have put up their own "Home Page."

Try to teach the exact same skills, using the exact same equipment, in a traditional school setting, and you'll have a year-long curriculum which will produce a healthy crop of failures.

What's wrong with this picture?

This chapter examines how—and why—our schools are doing exactly what they're designed to do: cause ADD children to fail. It will look at a variety of causes for both our schools' and our childrens' failures, from Napoleon's conquest of Prussia in 1806, to the loss of fiction-reading as a hobby, to the ways our gifted children are crushed by the weight of modern teaching institutions.

"Good German Schools" Come to America

The greatest thing in the world is to know how to belong to oneself. —Montaigne

Tens of millions of Americans now know how to use computers *without* having learned these skills in school. In fact, if they had learned how to use computers in school, they would probably be far less functional in their use of computers. Why? Because of the way schools are designed. They're not designed to teach, they're designed to condition.

While we have all heard about the hard school years in Japan, few know that children in Hong Kong's schools—with a shorter school year—regularly outperform Japanese students in both math and science. Or consider Sweden, one of the countries with the highest literacy rates in the world: Sweden doesn't send its children to school until they're seven years old, and Swedish high schools graduate children after nine instead of 12 years of schooling.

In May of 1996 Louise and I visited Taiwan and found that their public school system is shockingly different from that of America. We saw lot of what looked to us like "ADD behavior" among the Taiwanese: they are, after all, descendants of the malcontents who tried and failed to take over China, and then fled to Taiwan where they largely destroyed the indigenous people.

How do they handle ADD there? Their schools are high-stimulation places where these high-energy kids thrive.

Taiwanese schools are so high-stim that an article in *The Independent* in London on June 6, 1996, by Fran Abrams, referred to their classrooms as "anarchic." Children aren't required to sit quietly: instead, they're allowed to jump up from their seats to write on the board, to speak up, to shout out answers, all without waiting for permission from their teachers. Book-work constitutes less than a few minutes out of each 40-minute class session: most of the time is instead devoted to discussion and action. "And the Taiwanese pupils are ahead of their British counterparts," summarizes the article in *The Independent.*

School in the United States, on the other hand, has become a profitable monopoly even as the system itself is failing and collapsing. When schools do poorly, they get more funding: when they do well, nobody notices. What incentive do they have, then, to do well?

As Jaime Escalante and other "superstar" teachers have found out to their horror, American education is now part of and run as a medieval guild system, where no one is allowed to outperform or "show up" anybody else, no one is allowed to advertise or "become a star," and new technologies and improvisations are considered taboo without the approval of the guild.

To understand the origins of this system we have to go back to the last years of the 18th century. The state of Prussia (now part of Germany) had as a major industry the export of soldiers. If your country wanted to fight a war, you hired the Prussian experts to come in and show you how, and in many cases even fight it for you. The Prussian army was known and feared all across Europe.

Until 1806.

In that year, at the battle of Jena, Napoleon's amateur soldiers trounced the Prussian army, producing a profound and humiliating defeat for Prussia. Not only was the Prussian national pride at stake, but also their livlihood: their national business was producing and supplying soldiers and armies.

This defeat led the German philosopher Fichte to deliver what was to become one of the most powerful documents in the history of education: his "Address to the German Nation." In it, he blamed the defeat at Jena on soldiers who were not sufficiently willing to obey authority and take orders. He then proposed a system of forced education which would produce soldiers and citizens who would be obedient, well-behaved, unquestioning of authority, and who would share similar opinions (taught in the "schools") on issues of "national importance."

By 1819 the Prussian King had agreed with Fichte. He didn't want to lose any more wars. He ordered that all citizens must send their children to the new public school institution or face severe punishments. It was the world's first compulsory public school, and its agenda was not educational *per se* but the fulfillment of social/industrial/military goals.

This led to an explosion over the next decades in the wealth and success of Prussian industry and the Prussian military. Soldiers accepted orders, workers obeyed their managers, the Prussian government flourished, and the people of Prussia adopted similar viewpoints on all the issues identified as crucial by their King.

Elsewhere in the world, governments who were struggling with issues of nonconformity and rebellion were fascinated by the apparent success of the Prussian experiment.

Here in the United States during the early- and mid-1800s the benefits of this type of schooling were fiercely debated. On one -2side, wealthy owners of factories, mines, and farms argued strongly for such a system to provide them with more compliant workers. The westward expansion taking place at that time occasionally produced shortages of factory labor, and "independent American thinking" was viewed by these industrialists as a social ill.

On the other side of the argument were the post-Jeffersonians who believed that educational decisions about children should be made by those children's parents. If groups of parents or communities wanted to get together to hire a teacher and start a school, the structure of the classroom, the duration of the school year, and all the other aspects of education in their community should be up to them. The post-Jeffersonians believed that allowing communities this independence would create workable school systems and foster superior education.

The Prussian program had addressed this debate right from the start by creating a two-tiered school system which endures to this day in modern Germany. The Volksschule (people's school) educated over 90% of the country's children, in a way that was guaranteed to produce conformity, compliance, and to stifle independent thought. The Real Schulen (actual school) educated the remaining 8 to 10 percent of the students, the children of the ruling and wealthy elite, who were destined to become the leaders of government and industry.

Unfortunately for America, the debate was settled here by the resolution of "the Catholic problem" in the state of Massachusetts. In 1852 a Protestant secret society known as The Order of the Star Spangled Banner dominated Massachusetts politics. (Their password was the phrase: "I know nothing.") Their political arm, The American Party, controlled the Massachusetts legislature and was concerned about the Catholic immigrants from Ireland who were flooding the state and especially the port of Boston. That same year the famous "Know Nothing" legislature of Massachusetts (yes, it's referred to as that in the history books) passed a law designed to take young Catholic children away from their parents and indoctrinate them in the ways of the state. One of the unspoken goals was to Americanize these children, to displace the influence of Irish family culture. Compulsory public schooling had only once before been tried and was soon abandoned in this country—in the Massachusetts colony in 1650 by the witch-burners at Salem. Now it became state law, and soon other states across the country began to adopt the Massachusetts model.

And so began the dumbing down of America. Horace Mann went to Prussia to view the Teutonic school model and thought it wonderful: he came back to America and strongly advocated its widespread distribution as a way to cure our social ills, tame the wild west, and provide "educated" workers for industry. When the federal government finally got into the act, one of the first US Commissioners of Education, William Torrey Harris, went out of his way in 1889 to assure Collis Huntington, one of the fabulously wealthy railroad magnates of that day, that this new system of national compulsory education was scientifically designed to prevent "over-education" from happening to American children. There would always be a ready supply of drones to help build and maintain the railroads.

In addition to the dumbing down of American citizens, the Prussian model of Volksschule has, in the opinion of some, also led to two world wars. In the classic *All Quiet on the Western Front,* Erich Remarque asserts that World War One was caused "by the tricks of schoolmasters."

Even more chilling was the view of the famous Protestant theologian Dietrich Bonhoeffer who pointed out that World War Two was the "inevitable product" of this type of schooling and child raising. By that he meant was that the German people had, for several generations, been stripped of their critical thinking skills. They had, in his opinion, become a nation of good and obedient drones, who thought alike and were willing to follow the instructions of those in authority, regardless of how bizarre or immoral those orders might seem. They were ready to follow the rantings of a demagogue.

Hitler himself was a strong advocate of using compulsory public schools to socialize children. National Socialist (Nazi) philosophy was a compulsory part of school curriculum during his reign. It is also significant that in Hitler's Germany children were forced to attend school daily starting at age five.

So it should be no surprise to us that children are coming out of American public schools deprived of their critical thinking skills, and missing the ability to analyze complex problems or understand the details of far-reaching political issues. It shouldn't amaze us that Americans today—the products of years in a misbegotten school system—will march in lockstep enthusiasm to single-sentence political slogans dealing with complex issues such as flag-burning, abortion, the decriminalization of drugs and international trade.

What many of us don't know or have forgotten is that our system was designed from the ground up to operate exactly as it does today. Once upon a time the most important product of a public school system, for government and commerce, was compliant young women for the household and men for the army and industry. Do we still want this today?

This system has no provisions for talented children who are less than enthusiastic about sitting in the same room all day every day doing the same thing, from kindergarten through old age. Like

Robin Williams' character in *Good Morning Vietnam*—a heretic and misfit in a conformist system—they stick out and get in the way. So they are given pejorative labels as troublemaker or hyperactive or ADD and these days frequently are medicated with drugs like Ritalin to help them comply with the system. Sometimes this works, and these rebels and misfits become "good students," "good children," who behave and become "good citizens."

Solutions

Solutions to the problems of our schools are perhaps the most problematic of any in this book. In my opinion and experience, what's called for is a radical re-invention of our school systems. This would make them more functional and accessible for children with ADD, and also increase the quality and quantity of learning available to non-ADD children. The details could include:

• *Relevant curriculum.* Rudolph Steiner (after whose ideas the Waldorf Schools are patterned) had the idea that teaching should not be subject-specific, but multi-subject simultaneously. Have children write about History as part of their English curriculum. Do the Math to determine the accuracy of Einstein's Time Dilation Equation as part of Physics, and then write up a summary of it in German as part of their language lesson. Integrating subjects together, Steiner thought, would make education more relevant and more like the real world.

In fact, his idea wasn't anything new. It was the way that much instruction had been done for thousands of years, and it wasn't until the Prussian school model came along in the early 19th century that the idea that breaking up topics and dealing with each in a vacuum was considered. The reason for this was simple: the Prussian King wanted his students to be compartmentalized thinkers, unable to see the interconnectedness of things, and thus good cannon fodder.

• *Student participation in the educational process.* My youngest daughter (14) became interested in herbal medicine from reading old books we have around the house. This led her to study Latin, so she could understand the names of the plants, taxonomy so she could understand their classifications, botany so she could understand how they grew and formed healing compounds, and a whole spectrum of studies in human medicine from anatomy to physiology so she could understand their effects. Dad, what's a diuretic, and, if it's what I think it is, how do the kidneys effect blood pressure?" was this morning's question, followed an hour later by, Dad, what's the active alkaloid in Uva Ursi." A year ago she didn't know what the word alkaloid" meant: she's learned more, in a variety of disciplines, in the past year *outside of school* than she has in the previous two years of public schools, and it's all because she *wanted* to learn these things.

Many private schools are well-known for working with students to devise their own curriculum. The bottom line is that when kids want to learn something, you can't stop them. So the emphasis in our schools should shift from trying to force education on children to inspiring them to want it.

 • *Student empowerment in the classroom.* Most public-school classrooms are mini-autocracies. As such, they alienate the students from the teachers and vice-versa. At Horizon School in Atlanta, the public schools of Taiwan, and other private, alternative schools, the students help in defining the rules of classroom behavior, and there's far more emphasis on learning than on behaving. As a result, learning happens

 • *Recognize good teachers and pay them appropriately, while weeding out the dead wood.* When we begin to pay teachers the salaries we pay corporate executives, we'll begin producing students capable of becoming corporate executives. But the guild or union system that most public schools work under works actively against this, and even when the union is willing to participate the administration or school boards usually are not. We need to get rid of the layers of bureaucracy which are suffocating our good teachers and protecting our bad ones, and trust and empower those who really care so they can help our children learn.

 • *Break down the mandatory structures of education to open more alternatives.* Homeschooling, alternative schools, local community schools, Charter schools, and one-room schools all are viable alternatives to public education, but they're often fought by political or educational power structures. Decisions of these types rightly belong with parents and communities, not with the federal government, or even the state governments.

American Schools Focus on Content
Instead of Technique

"Don't talk to me about their test scores until we administer to their hearts."

—Melba Coleman, school principal

In 1986 my wife Louise and I lived for a year in a rural part of northern Bavaria. Our son, Justin, was then eight years old and in the second grade. None of his teachers could speak to him in English, so he quickly learned German, but the language difference wasn't half the shock to him (or my wife and me) that the school culture was.

After about a month in school, Louise was called by the teacher for an "urgent conference." She wanted her to come during the school day so she could see for herself the magnitude of the problem.

When Louise arrived at the elementary school, Justin's teacher met her at the office and took her up to the hall outside the classroom. Against the wall was a neat row of shoes, which each of the students had removed (it was winter). These were replaced with a pair of slippers the children wore when they entered the classroom. The row was perfectly neat, each pair of shoes in order and perpendicular to the wall, with one exception. Justin's shoes were slightly off-kilter, and one was turned on its side.

"Look at that!" his teacher hissed to Louise. "He can never keep his shoes straight."

They then walked into the classroom and the teacher marched over to Justin's desk, Louise in tow. The students were all reading. In the groove at the top of the wooden desk was the fountain pen we'd purchased for Justin on his first day of school. The teacher pointed to it. "The cap is facing left," she said in a stage whisper. "Notice that all the other students' pen's caps are facing right." She shook her head, angry and astounded by Justin's inability to master such matters. "He simply refuses to attend to these important details, and he also often has ink on his hands, desk, and shirt."

The final problem had to do with Justin's penmanship. While by second grade all the other students were proficient in cursive writing with a fountain pen, Justin had only mastered block letters with a pencil in the American second grade he'd attended the year earlier. "It's as if he's never been to school," the teacher said sadly.

Learning Skills

In 1913, Newson and Company was a major publisher of school textbooks. *Aldine's First Language Book* was the text for Grade Three and used by 8-year-olds in elementary schools across America. One of the early lessons contained twelve poems, one for each month. Here is November's, and the text that followed the twelve poems, addressed to the child.

November

Trees bare and brown,
Dry leaves everywhere,
Dancing up and down
Whirling through the air.
Red-cheeked apples roasted,
Popcorn almost done,
Toes and chestnuts toasted
That's November fun.

Learn by heart the quotation you like best or the one about your birth month. Read the whole quotation through, close your book, and try to say it to yourself. If you cannot, read it all through again, and again, until you can say it. Do not try to learn it line by line. That breaks up the poem and destroys the beauty of it. Always read it all and try to say it all.

When you are sure you know it, write it from memory. After you have finished writing, open your book and compare the quotation as you have written it with the quotation as it is in the book. Correct any mistakes you have made. If you really try to do your best work, you should have very few mistakes in the first writing, and you should be able to find and correct these without any help from your teacher.

What we see in both the German school example, and in *Aldine's First Language Book*, is an emphasis on learning *skills every bit as important as the emphasis on content or information. Children are taught to be organized, to do things in what's considered the proper fashion, and given instruction in specific techniques, such as how to properly memorize a poem.*

An Atlanta teacher who asked that I not quote her by name said, "We are so driven these days by tests and scores, by standardized levels of achievement, that we have little time to handle what I'd consider the basics: how to study, how to learn, how to get organized and do your homework. Classrooms are viewed as places to impart information, and therefore we've lost the concept of mentorship, of teaching *skills.* Education should be about lighting the fire of interest which will burn for the rest of the child's life, but instead we've made it just the filling of the bucket of a white-bread curriculum."

So kids don't do well in school, or they learn the information but never master the techniques, and then the day comes when they must know the techniques and they crash and burn. And some are diagnosed as having ADD, when actually their biggest problem is a lack of study skills.

Solutions

Let's examine the ways our schools are organized, and the content of what they teach, to emphasize life and educational skill building before worrying about content. When children understand *how* to learn, then the learning usually follows.

Our Gifted Kids are Bored Silly

"Geniuses used to be rare. Today, thanks to popular inter-pretation of test scores, every elementary or secondary school has its quota."

—John W. Gardner, *EXCELLENCE:*
Can we be equal and excellent too?

It not surprising that it would take *Forbes*, the magazine that for years had as its slogan "Capitalist Tool," to point out that the way money is spent in the field of education is truly bizarre. In a recent issue, an article by Peter Brimelow asks the question: "Would any management worth a damn put most of its dollars into its weakest divisions and starve the promising ones of capital?"

The next sentence answers: "Not and live for long."

Yet, as the article goes on to show in eloquent detail, that is exactly what is happening with funding for our brightest and most gifted children in the U.S. educational system. According to the Department of Education, state and local spending on gifted and talented children is less than two cents per hundred dollars spent. And federal funding for gifted children is never more than one-tenth of one percent.

According to the Department of Education, this is the way federal spending on education in 1993 was allocated:

49.8% to "Disadvantaged" ($6.9 billion)

30.13% to "Other" including bilingual, vocational, & impact aid ($4.1 billion)

20.0% to "Handicapped" ($2.8 billion)

00.07% to "Gifted" ($.0096 billion)

What makes this so very distressing is the number of children who are labeled as ADD but who are also gifted or have above-average intelligence.

James T. Webb and Diane Latimer in a recent issue of the ERIC Digest, list the entire diagnostic criteria for ADHD in the American Psychiatric Association's Diagnostic and Statistical Manual, Version Three, Revised (DSM-IIIR), and then follow it with: "Almost all of these behaviors, however, might be found in bright, talented, creative, gifted children."

The specific behavioral characteristics associated with giftedness that Webb identifies are:

1. Poor attention, boredom, daydreaming in specific situations.
2. Low tolerance for persistence on tasks that seem irrelevant.
3. Judgment lags behind development of intellect.
4. Intensity may lead to power struggles with authorities.
5. High activity level; may need less sleep.
6. Questions rules, customs and traditions.

Compare those with Russell Barkley's 1990 list of behaviors associated with ADHD from his "Attention Deficit Hyperactivity Disorder: A Handbook for Diagnosis and Treatment," as summarized by Webb, et al:

1. Poorly sustained attention in almost all situations.
2. Diminished persistence on tasks not having immediate consequences.
3. Impulsivity, poor delay of gratification.
4. Impaired adherence to commands to regulate or inhibit behavior in social contexts.
5. More active, restless, than normal children.
6. Difficulty adhering to rules and regulations.

Which brings us back to our schools. For bright children there's often only a subtle distinction between giftedness and ADD, and gifted kids are often misdiagnosed as having ADD/ADHD. Rarely, however, are ADD kids diagnosed as being gifted. Even worse, children who are both gifted and ADD are almost always merely diagnosed as having ADD while their giftedness is ignored.

Therapist Lamar Waldron is fond of pointing out that people will almost always frame problems in terms of the tools or experience they can offer as solutions. ("When the only tool you have is a hammer, everything in the world looks like a nail.") Drug addiction, for example, is viewed by a physician as a medical problem, while a police officer sees it as a criminal problem. Over 80% of our national school resources for special education are for the handicapped, slower, less functional, retarded, or learning disabled children. Since less than one percent is for gifted children, it should be of no surprise to anybody that the standard school response to a gifted ADD child is to treat the ADD and ignore the giftedness. Adding insult to injury, many gifted ADD children find themselves as a result of their ADD diagnosis, in a slower-than-normal classroom environment, since they've been identified as having a "learning disability."

Webbs, et al, point out that in a typical classroom, a gifted child may spend one-fourth to one-half of their entire time simply waiting for others to catch up. "Such children often respond to non-challenging or slow-moving classroom situations by 'off-task' behavior, disruptions, or other attempts at self-amusement. This use of extra time is often the cause of the referral for an ADHD evaluation."

And, in a rather depressing conclusion, they say, "Do not be surprised if the professional [to whom you're referred for the ADHD evaluation] has little training in recognizing the characteristics of gifted/talented children."

Bright children with ADD are often not identified as having ADD until the fourth- through ninth-grade levels. This is because they can usually maintain grade-level work with a minimum amount of effort, and don't "crash and burn" until they hit a grade level or classroom where a high level of performance is required. By this time, however, they've developed a lifetime of skills to just get by, and have missed learning critical study-habit skills, usually absorbed by normal children in the middle elementary years. The result is that the child's old strategies don't work, and there are no fallback strategies to call upon.

This explains, in part, both the proliferation and the success of the study skill classes that so many private tutoring institutions are offering; these are popping up like dandelions in middle and upper-middle-class neighborhoods. They teach children in junior and senior high school the basic study skills that their peers acquired in elementary school, but that they missed.

Those children who are most in need of these skills to make it through boring, mandatory classes, or when they hit challenging, demanding classes—have also missed out on the early-years opportunity to integrate these organizational and study skills seamlessly into their personality. Even when they learn how to organize their materials, learn how to study, etc., these skills are not yet habits. They're not supported by years of practice and reinforcement, and are so far from second-nature that they seem counterintuitive to the child.

And so we see a consistent unevenness in the ability of these kids to keep it together in school. They attend the study skills class, and their grades shoot up for a month or two. Then they crash and burn and need another dose of technique reminders, all largely because in elementary school their abilities weren't recognized. The schools don't usually have specific programs for the gifted even if they had identified them.

The schools' response to this situation has been to encourage the use of medication and support groups, essentially pointing the finger of blame at the victims, instead of acknowledging the responsibility of an incompetent educational system.

In fact the problem for these bright children is often primarily in the structure of the schools. With less than 1% of total federal and state monies going to programs for gifted children, it's small wonder that so many psychologists and psychiatrists marvel at the high number of very bright children being referred to them for ADD diagnoses from the public schools.

Medication, Smaller Classes

Further evidence of this situation can be seen from the results that private schools can obtain with children who have failed in the public schools. There is no doubt that medication can produce a huge difference in a child's performance in a public school setting, but many private schools obtain similar results by simply using smaller classes. This instruction moves at a pace commensurate with the child's ability to learn, and the teaching is in an active, visual, hands-on fashion consistent with an ADD child's learning style.

During the "Ritalin scare" of 1993, stocks of the drug were depleted nationwide. Parents across the country petitioned government agencies and called their congresspersons and senators to demand that Ritalin be reclassified as a Class III controlled substance, easing up on its being lumped into the Class II category along with pharmaceutical cocaine and morphine.

How many of those parents, however, ever bothered to call or write to demand that our schools challenge our children to learn? How many asked that funding for bright children be increased from .07% to some higher number?

The vast majority of parents reading this are probably parents of children who are both ADD and of above-average intelligence. There's a self-selection process that's hard to avoid. Those parents who make the effort to find, buy and read a book tend to be higher in income, and usually higher in intelligence than the average. Such parents tend to produce above-average-intelligence offspring.

Over and over again on the ADD Forum on CompuServe we see parents complaining that their ADD-diagnosed children are acting-out in school more out of boredom than anything else. "My son reads five grade levels above his class," one parent commented. "He spends most of his time in class trying to sit quietly while the teacher is holding the hands of the slower students. It's no wonder he gets bored and fidgets."

The teacher's prescription, of course, was to medicate this woman's son. While that would have helped him sit in his seat for the entire class day, and thereby increased his grade scores, it would have done nothing to address the fact he was ready to learn more than the teacher was able or willing to offer.

There was a brief window during the late 1950s and early 1960s when America was shocked by the Soviet Union's successful launch of the world's first artificial satellite, Sputnik. As a result, numerous programs for gifted children were instituted in elementary and secondary schools across the country. There was a refreshing new emphasis on experimenting with new teaching styles, and teaching more of the hard sciences at early ages.

Unfortunately, the Vietnam War brought an end to virtually all of those programs, as national resources were siphoned away from education and moved toward the military. Today, the cost of a single B-2 bomber aircraft is greater than the entire national expenditure on programs for gifted children from 1970 to 1993 *combined.*

Again, this is not a diatribe against medication or funding the military. The point is that our values have become scrambled over the past three decades. Private schools and home schooling are exploding in popularity because they're filling a huge void left by public schools: educational opportunity for gifted children.

As Brimelow points out in *Forbes*: "So the problem appears to be a classic one in economics: Resources are limited—where should they be allocated to get the best return?"

So here again we see some children are identified as being distractible and impulsive: they're too intelligent for their grade level and our educational system offers them no options. In short, they're bored silly.

Solutions

Programs for gifted children need the levels of funding they enjoyed during the Kennedy administration, before they were slashed to pay for the Vietnam war and never revived. This is an area where parents can advocate on levels from the local school board all the way to their Congressperson, Senator, and the President.

Education is More Important Today than in Years Past

Education is the best provision for old age.
                              —Aristotle, 384-322 B.C.

Fifty years ago the percentage of children graduating from high school was much lower than it is today.

A high school diploma wasn't considered "necessary" for many occupations, particularly those involving manual labor, farm, or factory work. It wasn't uncommon for people to enter the work force full-time at the age of 14 or 15, as did Thomas Edison. It was most likely the ADD individuals who dropped out of school and ended up working or joining the military at young ages.

Yet in those days—indeed, even as recently as twenty years ago—these people weren't considered odd or dysfunctional. They merely had chosen one particular career path, that of driving a taxi, or working in a factory or on a farm. (And this is very much still the case in Europe, where going into a trade school and doing an apprenticeship to be a baker, mechanic, or chef is considered highly respectable.)

I remember growing up in a working-class neighborhood, where several of my friends' parents worked at the local Oldsmobile plant. Many had never finished high school; some were European immigrants who spoke broken English. A willingness to work hard and membership in the union were their tickets to success, not education.

But today more children are staying in school longer. There's more pressure for them to stay in school, and fewer opportunities for those who drop out. I doubt most factories will even consider a job applicant without a high school diploma, for example, and even people applying for minimum-wage service-industry jobs find their resumes being scrutinized and themselves ranked by their high-school grades. This emphasis on staying in school, and on succeeding in school, creates more of an opportunity for children's ADD to be noticed, diagnosed, and treated. It also can lead to a near-hysteria among parents about their children's educational achievement.

Consider the grandest paradox: if ADD is genetically transmitted, why is it that the highest rates of diagnosis and treatment for it are usually in upper-middle-class white neighborhoods? Could it be that this is a condition that's only transmitted among upper-income people of European ancestry? Most geneticists would laugh at such a notion.

The obvious reasons are that such parents are more aware of the importance of education and therefore more sensitive to their children's school performance. In addition, children in upper-middle-class neighborhoods have better access to health-care professionals who can diagnose ADD and prescribe medications.

The Medication of Children

But even setting aside considerations of income or class, there are still powerful reasons for a school to want to label and/or medicate a child.

When I was executive director of a residential treatment facility for abused children in New Hampshire, I remember one boy who was brought into our program from the state mental hospital. He'd spent the past several years in the hospital, drugged with the powerful antipsychotic Thorazine into a dull stupor.

After withdrawing him from the drug and running a few month's worth of tests on him, our psychiatrist determined that he was neither psychotic nor even particularly neurotic, other than from the psychic pain he'd experienced from being locked up in a mental hospital for two years. He'd been dumped there as an emergency placement for a day to get him away from an abusive home because there were no beds that day in more appropriate places. Subsequently his case paperwork was lost or his social worker quit her job or something happened (we never did find out what) and he simply was kept there for a few years. This boy was locked into a little room, often tied to his bed, and, finally, continually drugged.

I asked his new social worker, who'd rescued him from the mental hospital and moved him to our program, why he'd been on Thorazine all that time. Her reply was both cynical and accurate: "With all the financial cutbacks in social services, the hospital was in a crisis. They were overworked and understaffed. So drugging him to passivity was probably the easiest, cheapest, and least troublesome way to handle him."

When I travel around the country speaking on ADD, frequently teachers are in the audience. Many have come up afterward to talk with me, and I've done seminars and trainings specifically for teachers and school administrators.

In all of these contacts, one distressingly familiar theme keeps reappearing. Our schools and teachers are overloaded and under-funded; they're not supported in their efforts by parents; and the most common scapegoats, those who have the finger of blame pointed at them when children fail, are the teachers.

This is, of course, totally unfair. While there are some teachers who are just putting in their time, the vast majority are committed, caring professionals who are trying to do their best in a world of diminishing resources and increasing demands.

Part of the solution to this problem, for many teachers and schools, has been the diagnosis of ADD. By identifying and treating children with ADD several things happen which from the school's point of view are desirable.

First, the blame for the child's failure to perform at the level of his or her potential is shifted from the teacher to the child. It's not that the teacher is overloaded, or under-funded, or even incompetent—it's that the child has a deficit in his ability to pay attention. Of course he's not learning: he has a neurological disorder.

Second, by medicating or otherwise treating the child to reduce his or her ADD-like behaviors (particularly those which are hyperactive as well), the level of disruption in the already strained-to-capacity classroom is diminished. This also benefits the teacher and the school. (It has the added benefit of improving the probability that students will be able to learn, but that's a point to reference later.)

While far less Dickensian than the experience of our child referred from the state mental hospital, the root cause is the same, as is the potential for abuse. The simple fact is that schools and teachers are hitting levels of overload. Add to this the shrill voices among the middle-and upper-middle-class, shouting about the inadequacy of the schools, and politicians calling for privatization of schools, vouchers, and all the rest. It's both convenient and useful to label, blame, and medicate students rather than paying to teach them.

Solutions

Let's work with our schools to give them better tools and better funding before we blame our children for their apparent inability to learn in a flawed and under-funded system.

Visual Learners in Auditory Schools

To see a world in a grain of sand,
And a heaven in a wild flower,
Hold infinity in the palm of your hand,
And eternity in an hour.
— William Blake, *Auguries of Innocence*

Leif Roland is one of the most effective psychologists I know. He runs Gestalt and NLP therapy groups, does individual therapy in Atlanta, and is solidly grounded in the notion that people are individuals and not labels.

Over lunch in November of 1995, Leif presented to me a startling and fascinating view of one possible reason for why we have ADD.

"I grew up in Denmark in the 1950s," Leif said. "My parents told me stories and read to me. In school we read constantly, and for recreation at night at home we'd either read or listen to the radio.

"As a consequence, I'm a very competent auditory learner. When I hear things, I'm quite good at understanding them and processing the information within them. When I'm doing therapy, I find it easy to listen to a person and discover what they're really saying, what their deeper levels of meaning are. I can hear subtleties in their tone of voice that others may miss, for example, and this is useful in my work.

"But what I'm seeing increasingly among my clients is that more and more people, particularly here in America, are visual learners. They don't listen well, or at least don't understand or process what they're hearing, but instead they use their eyes to experience and learn from the world."

After that lunch with Leif, I went home and dug out a picture book of *The New York Times* which dated back to the last century. Reading articles written a hundred years ago, I was struck by how detailed they were, how linear and methodical, and how turgid was the writing style.

My father had given me some textbooks he'd kept from high school in the 1940s, and I dug them out. His 7th grade history text would intimidate a modern college freshman. The tests in his 8th grade English textbook would overwhelm most college graduates I've interviewed for employment in the past ten years (and there have been dozens, if not over a hundred).

The Conservative Curmudgeon view of this transition in education is that our schools have become more permissive, weaker in their emphasis on learning, and less willing or able to discipline, threaten, or force children to learn. This has spawned a back-to-the-basics movement that's most visible in the Christian schools and military academies, but even there the levels of academic achievement which were the norms in 1920 are rarely achieved.

Certainly modern children have more distractions and more alternatives to paying attention in school. There is TV, movies, the mall, the mobility of automobiles, and all the many lures of modern society (many provided by companies with a specific profit/sales agenda). There's also an increased lack of parental involvement in the educational process as more parents are divorcing or both parents must work to maintain a middle-class lifestyle.

But many educators say these simple answers couldn't possibly be at the real core of modern children's relative inability to learn in the classroom. "It's gotta be something deeper, something more structural within the brain," one Southern California teacher told me when we were discussing this after a lecture I'd given in suburban Los Angeles. "These kids are somehow fundamentally different from the way I was and from the way my parents were."

Could it be that this difference is real, and that what it's really about is the transition people are making from an auditory to a visual learning style?

While some educators point to the 1960s as the time when our schools "collapsed" or became too permissive, that period of time also coincides with the first generation of children raised with TV.

So much of our information now comes to us visually. More than two decades ago, television replaced newspapers as the primary way most people obtain their news. About that time studies began to show that children spent more time watching TV than they did interacting with their family or their peers.

Print media has become more visual: *USA Today* is sometimes referred to by old-school newspaper reporters as "TV journalism in print," and probably the publishers wouldn't altogether disavow that appellation. The news is presented in highly visual, easily digested bytes, perfect for both the busy executive and the attention-span-deficient person.

Advertising, compared with 40 years ago, is wildly more visual and less verbal. Rare are the ads with more than a few paragraphs of copy, whereas ads from the last century were often nothing but words. Best-selling books are translated into movies to reach wider audiences: that simple transition can increase dramatically the audience for a writer's work.

Even the nature of best-selling books has changed. John Saul's and Tom Clancy's books are highly visual and easy to read and sell in the millions. On the other hand, do you know anybody who has chosen to take Melville or Joyce or Dostyevsky with him or her for vacation reading? If even one name comes to mind, that's no doubt the proverbial exception that proves the rule: writing that has depth is no longer popular with the masses.

Both our society and the world in general are becoming more visual. But many of our institutions, particularly our schools, have not kept up. Our educational institutions were developed over hundreds (in some cases, thousands) of years during which the oral, and then the written, tradition reigned. We moved from telling stories around the fire to lecturing in class. Speech-making is still the primary educational model, augmented by reading assignments—all auditory teaching methods.

Yet the children who are in these school and college class-rooms are now conditioned virtually from birth to learn by visual means. The result is that while the teacher is speaking English (at least in American schools), it may as well be Greek, because after ten or fifteen minutes the auditory-learning attention-span has been exceeded and the child is no longer paying attention.

Until our children are again taught to be good auditory processors (not likely to happen in any home that has a TV), or our educational institutions begin to offer far more visual and stimulating forms of education (not likely to happen in these days of budget crises), there will continue to be an epidemic of children who seemingly just can't learn. And they are often diagnosed as having ADD.

Solutions

Read to your children, from birth to their teenage years. Reduce the amount of TV that your kids are allowed to watch. And engage them in conversation whenever possible, challenging them to think and reason.

We Now See More ADD Because
of Standardized Curriculum

"Irresponsibility is part of the pleasure of all art, it is the part the schools cannot recognize."

—Pauline Kael

This chapter posits that the reason why we're seeing so much ADD diagnosed in our public schools (and, as adults, in the workplace) is because of a standardized school curriculum and similarly structured workplaces.

A few years ago I heard a fellow who was ridiculing the idea that there may be such a thing as ADD point out that "there is no ADD in front of a video game." He went on to conclude that "if ADD goes away in one environment, like the video arcade, but appears in another environment, like the school, then where is the real problem? Is it in the person or the environment?"

While this argument was meant to imply that there's no such thing as ADD, it suffers from a basic flaw in logic. Virtually all children can be transfixed by a video game, yet only a minority (albeit a substantial and growing one) are unable to succeed in school because of attentional problems. This implies some sort of fragility in their attentional structure or ability to learn that simply doesn't show up in front of a video game, but becomes apparent in the classroom; it doesn't indicate that there's no such thing as ADD.

A fascinating but largely overlooked study was published in 1983 that measured how far a child with ADD could be pushed—with and without medication—to do unfamiliar schoolwork. They found that if the amount of unfamiliar material a child was asked to learn or read exceeded the 15% to 30% range, then ADD children experienced a breakdown in their ability to complete tasks, to stay on-task, and to comprehend the material. When they were given stimulant medication, their ability to stay on-task dramatically improved and there was a slight improvement in their task comprehension, but their ability to complete tasks actually dropped.

The startling part, however, came when they changed the difficulty of the schoolwork. Shifting the percentage of new material to the 3% to 7% range, suddenly all the ADD children's ADD school problems vanished—both when they were medicated and when they were not.

Non-ADD children were equally able to handle the 30% new material and the 7% new material, but ADD kids needed medication to make the transition into the more difficult classroom. On the other hand, when the ADD children were allowed to move ahead at their own pace, keeping a daily 3% to 7% new material learned rate, they did as well as, and in some cases better than, their "normal" peers.

The Results of the Study

First, ADD kids have a more fragile learning style. They can handle learning as well as anybody, but only so long as their frustration level isn't exceeded. This means that in a classroom where instruction is individualized and/or the children are able to determine their own pace, ADD children didn't have a problem: they are able to perform as well as other children. Experience with alternative schools where children set their own pace, home schooling, and one-room schoolhouses where the wide variety of grade levels requires that each student move at his own pace, all bear this out: ADD isn't a significant problem in these environments.

When ADD children are confronted with high frustration levels, however, either from too much or too little new material, then ADD manifests. Because our schools now have an increasing emphasis on standardization of curriculum and scores (with teachers measured on their ability to keep children within these "norms"), it's not surprising that we see so much ADD suddenly popping up. The classroom environment is almost designed to bring it out: Johnny's way ahead of his class, and therefore bored/frustrated, in English, while he's overwhelmed/frustrated in Algebra. In neither case can he control the level of challenge or speed, or amount of information that's being thrown at him. In both cases he will crash and burn.

Second, this study points out that while the medication helps children with staying on-task, it's not doing much at all for their comprehension. But since class-work and homework require staying on-task behavior, and are the primary measurements of grades, medication seems to have a significant and positive effect on a child's ability to perform in school. It's important to note, though, that when the medication was withdrawn and the frustration level was brought down from 30% to 7%, these ADD children performed more than twice as well, medicated or not, in the area of comprehension.

In other words, management and customization of curriculum to keep daily frustration levels above 3% and below 7% has more than twice the positive effect on an ADD child's ability to learn than does their taking medication.

It's unlikely, however, that this is going to happen anytime soon in our schools. In order to process the largest number of students through the system with the greatest efficiency at the lowest cost, every one must be plugged into a standardized slot, regardless of his or her particular level of comprehension or ability. And this, of course, is a prescription for disaster for ADD children.

While I know of no similar studies done on adults, it's probably reasonable to conclude that an adult with ADD would not have a problem if their job and life situation offered a reasonable but not excessive amount of challenge and stimulation. On the other hand, if they were confronted with continual boredom, or with challenges which overwhelmed them, they'd probably begin to fail in the ways that are classically described in the literature.

Solutions

Parents can and should work with the schools to provide more diversity in their curriculum and their teaching methods.

When that's not available, political action from the local to the national level may be useful. In addition, tutoring, home-schooling, or placing children in a private school have all proved to be viable alternatives to allowing kids to fail in the public schools.

Our Children are Losing Empathy Abilities

The heavens laugh with you in your jubilee;
My heart is at your festival,
My head hath its coronal,
The fullness of your bliss I feel– I feel it all.
—William Wordsworth, 1770-1850, *Intimations of Mortality*

Criminologists note that two of the fastest growing segments of the criminal population are teen and pre-teen murderers. Children increasingly are being convicted of some of the most heinous crimes imaginable, and one of the shocking qualities of these young killers, robbers, and rapists is that they often express no remorse whatever for their crimes. They lack empathy, the ability to imagine what it must be like to be another person, to live within another person's skin, to feel the feelings that another person might have.

Startling evidence of this is found in the 1996 report of the U.S. Justice Department, which found that murders committed by teenagers in the United States had *tripled* in just ten years. The number of teenagers using guns to commit murder had *quadrupled*.

This is of concern since both children and adults with ADD often score low on tests that measure empathy. And the trend seems to be increasing: children are more likely to be non-empathetic than are their equally-ADD parents. Some psychologists speculate that they'll also grow up to be less empathetic adults than their parents (although at this moment no studies of this have been done that I could find.)

Why would this be?

So far, no one has offered a reasonable explanation, other than to note the fact that children and adults with ADD are often less empathetic than their non-ADD peers.

I believe, however, that there is a cause. It's specific and definable, and when considered carefully makes perfect sense. When I first thought of this I was in California at dinner, before giving a speech to an ADD support group. So I bounced the idea off two psychologists and a psychiatrist who had joined us at dinner. All thought it had merit, so I shared it with others, got similar responses, and now I offer it up for your consideration.

The Loss of Fiction

To have and express empathy requires that a person has had opportunities in life to imagine what it's like to be another person. While some may say this is an inborn characteristic, studies of sociopaths who grew up in violently abusive situations, and animal studies (yes, animals can show empathy, particularly primates), indicate that to a large extent empathy is learned.

So how and where and when do we learn empathy?

Certainly to some extent it's learned in the family, observing how parents and siblings express their feelings and hearing them tell stories of how they feel or how they reacted to certain situations. But in our modern TV-driven society, this type of interaction is diminishing.

Another source of empathy-learning opportunity comes from peer groups, although children are notoriously cruel and pre-empathetic. While peer-group interaction provides an important opportunity for children to learn empathy, it may not be the most important. And when the peer groups themselves are based in non-empathetic behaviors (such as gangs), peer groups may actually serve to either deter the learning of empathy or to cause children or adults to suppress empathetic behaviors.

Television, the movies, and the theater all seem as if they would represent opportunities for children to learn empathy, but in fact none offers the opportunity to really get inside another person's skin. We can observe people's reactions in these media, but we don't know what they're really thinking.

Only fiction, principally in the form of the novel, offers the opportunity to get inside the mind of another person.

While it's true that our internal world literally ends at the edge of our skin, with a well-written novel the reader actually has an opportunity to vicariously inhabit the body and mind and soul of another human being. Novels don't just show action and dialogue like TV and movies; they present thoughts. The reader knows what the scene looks like not because of the novelist's description, but because the skillful novelist shows us what *the character* is seeing, hearing, feeling, smelling, and tasting. When reading a well-written novel, we're actually inside the mind of another person, we sense the world with their senses, feel their reactions, and know their thoughts.

This is a powerful tool to teach and build empathy.

For the first hundred millennia of human history this was played out by oral tradition. Zog sat around the campfire and regaled the tribe with tales of his ancestors or of his hunt, how he felt, what he saw, how terrified he was as the tiger chased him through the forest. With the advent of written language and then the printing press, the oral tradition was replaced by the written word and then the book. For the past five or six thousand years this was the main way stories were told and empathy was taught.

Then came television.

Numerous researchers have chronicled the rise in television viewing since it spread like Kudzu across the American landscape in the 1950s. They've noted over and over again that the more television children watch, the less likely they are to perform well academically, and the less likely they are to read recreationaly. Marie Winn, author of *The Plug-In Drug*, and others have carefully chronicled the positive correlation between TV watching and criminal behavior, particularly violent behavior. Many point to the *content* of the TV shows as feeding violent instincts and tendencies.

But literature and oral tradition have been filled with violence for nearly all of human history. The Bible, for example, has books within it that chapter one gory story of mass murder after another, along with rules of behavior which have death as the penalty for breaking. Traditional fairy tales and children's stories are filled with violence. TV may be drenching children with violence, or at least educating them how to be violent, but it may not be as responsible for the loss of empathy as is the loss of what TV has come to replace: reading.

This is not to suggest that ADD is caused by people not reading, but some symptoms and co-morbidities, particularly lack of empathy and poor academic skills, certainly could be.

Reading is a focusing exercise, training young brains to maintain their attention on a single thing for a long period of time. Unlike TV, which has fast-moving images and therefore does not train a longer attention span, reading requires effort, thus training the brain in this regard.

Reading is an academic exercise. It trains the processing of language into visual imagery which is so essential to functional long-term memory, and with practice people learn to read faster and faster. This, of course, can only benefit schoolwork.

Finally, reading is an empathy exercise. When a child is reading *Tom Sawyer* or a teenager is reading one of Parker's Spenser novels, they are engaging in the core-activity of empathy: vicariously experiencing the life of another.

But there's a chicken-and-egg phenomenon at work here. Children with ADD are less likely to become excited about reading at a young age, perhaps because of ADD as a learning disability or perhaps because our schools are so poorly set up to teach ADD children to read. Whatever the cause, the effect is that kids with ADD tend to read less well, and so recreational reading is difficult for them. This difficulty means they often don't become hooked on reading fiction at a young age, and may grow into adulthood without ever having read anything not required by school. Because they're not reading recreationaly, they're not improving their reading skills, making recreational reading an ongoing difficulty.

Try an experiment. Ask several of the ADD children or adults you know how many novels they've read in their lives, and in the past few years. Then ask yourself which of these people seems the most capable or incapable of showing or experiencing empathy. I predict that your results will be the same as were mine when I did this: the less fiction a person reads, the less empathetic they often appear and may, in fact, be.

Solutions

Read to children. Get them addicted to good fiction. It may take having them listen to books on tape during a long trip in the car, or reading to them every night before bed. Read instead of watching TV as a family activity: all these are ways to get kids hooked on fiction.

CHAPTER THREE

Genetics and Psychology

Could it be that ADD is something that was once useful for the human race, but is now—particularly in schools—a liability? Or that Abraham Maslow, the founder of Humanistic Psychology, overlooked a "basic human need" which provides us with a key to understanding the mechanism which underlies ADD?

Rich in scientific insight and pushing the barriers of contemporary thinking about ADD, this chapter examines several possible reasons why ADD is so prevalent in our gene pool, and why stimulant drugs diminish its symptoms.

Starting with Hunters/Farmers and ending with the theory of thalamic gain, if you're scientifically inclined you'll probably find this one of the most fascinating chapters of this book.

ADD Characteristics—Leftover Hunter Genes

The creatures that want to live a life of their own, we call wild. If wild, then no matter how harmless, we treat them as outlaws, and those of us who are 'specially well brought up shoot them for fun.

—Clarence Day, *This Simian World,* 1920

The National Institutes of Mental Health (NIMH) have shown that the brains of people with ADD have a different type of glucose metabolism, or at least a different rate of blood flow, from those without ADD. This validates the neurological/physiological basis of ADD, but doesn't explain what it is, how it works, or where it came from. Similarly, researchers at the University of Chicago believe they've come close to isolating the gene responsible for ADD, but they can't say exactly how that gene affects the brain, or how or why it came to be part of our genetic makeup.

Theories abound positing neurotransmitter imbalances, frontal lobe abnormalities, blood-flow differences, and even the influence of excessive television viewing as a contributor to ADD, but, at this moment, nobody knows for sure exactly what ADD is or the mechanism by which it works.

At its core, ADD is generally acknowledged to have three components: *distractibility, impulsivity,* and *risk-taking/restlessness.* If you throw in hyperactivity, you have ADHD-Attention Deficit Hyperactive Disorder—which, until recently, was considered to be "true" ADD, but now is viewed as a separate condition. ADHD is the disorder that children were believed to grow out of sometime around adolescence, but it appears that most ADHD kids simply become adults with ADD, as the hyperactivity of their youth sometimes diminishes.

Distractibility

Distractibility is often mischaracterized as the inability of a child or adult to pay attention to a specific thing. Yet people with ADD *can* pay attention, even for long periods of time (it's called "hyperfocusing"), but only to something that excites or interests them. It's a cliché—but true—that "there is no ADD in front of a good video game."

ADD experts often noted it's not that ADDers can't pay attention to anything, it's that they pay attention to *everything*.

A better way to characterize the distractibility of ADD is to describe it as *scanning*. In a classroom, the child with ADD is the one who notices the janitor mowing the lawn outside the window, when he should be focusing on the teacher's lecture on long division. Likewise, the bug crawling across the ceiling, or the class bully preparing to throw a spitball, are infinitely more fascinating than the teacher's analysis of Columbus' place in history.

While this constant scanning of the environment is a liability in a classroom setting, it may have been a survival skill for our prehistoric ancestors.

A primitive hunter who didn't find that he easily and normally fell into a mental state of constant scanning would be at a huge disadvantage. That flash of motion on the periphery of his vision might be either the rabbit that he needed for lunch, or the tiger or bear hoping to make lunch of him. If he were to focus too heavily on the trail, for example, and therefore miss the other details of his environment, he would either starve or be eaten.

On the other hand, when the agricultural revolution began 12,000 years ago, this scanning turned into a liability for those people whose societies changed from hunting to farming. If the day came when the moon was right, the soil was the perfect moisture, and the crops due to be planted, a farmer couldn't waste his day wandering off into the forest to check out something unusual he noticed. He must keep his attention focused on the task at hand, and not be distracted from it.

Impulsivity

The characteristic of impulsivity has two core manifestations among modern people with ADD. The first is impulsive behavior: the proverbial acting-without-thinking-things-through. Often this takes the form of interrupting others or blurting things out in conversation. Other times it's reflected in snap judgments or quick decisions. ˙

A prehistoric hunter would describe impulsivity as an asset because it provided him with the ability to act on instant decisions, as well as the willingness to explore new and untested areas. If he were chasing a rabbit through the forest with his spear, and a deer ran by, he wouldn't have time to stop and calculate a risk/benefit analysis. He must make an instant decision about which animal to pursue, then act on that decision without a second thought.

Thomas Edison eloquently described how his combined distractibility and impulsiveness helped him in his "hunt" for world-transforming inventions. He said, "Look, I start here with the intention of going there" (drawing an imaginary line) "in an experiment, say, to increase the speed of the Atlantic cable; but when I have arrived part way in my straight line, I meet with a phenomenon and it leads me off in another direction, to something totally unexpected."

The second aspect of impulsivity is impatience. For a primitive farmer, however, impatience and impulsivity would be a disaster. If he were to go out into the field and dig up the seeds every day to see if they were growing, the crops would die. (The contemporary manifestation of this is the person who can't leave the oven door shut, but has to keep opening it to check how the food's doing, to the detriment of many a soufflé.) ˙

A very patient approach, all the way down to the process of picking bugs off plants for hours each day, day after day, would have to be hard-wired into the brain of a farmer. The word "boring" couldn't be in his vocabulary. His brain would have to be built in such a way that it tolerated, or even enjoyed, sticking with something until it was finished.

Restlessness

Risk-taking, or, as described in their book, *Driven to Distrac-*

tion, by Drs. Hallowell and Ratey, "a restive search for high stimulation," is perhaps the most destructive of the behaviors associated with ADD in contemporary society. It probably accounts for the high percentage of people with ADD among the prison populations, and plays a role in a wide variety of social problems, from the risky driving of a teenager to the infidelity or job-hopping of an adult.

Yet for a primitive hunter, risk and high-stimulation were a necessary part of daily life. If hunters were risk-or adrenaline-averse, they'd never go into the wilds to hunt. For a hunter, the idea of daily risking one's life would have to feel "normal." In fact, the urge to experience risk, the desire for that adrenaline high, would be necessary among the members of a hunting society, because it would propel their members out into the forest or jungle in search of stimulation and dinner.

If a farmer were a risk-taker, however, the results could lead to starvation. Because decisions made by farmers have such long-ranging consequences, their brains must be wired to avoid risks and to carefully determine the most risk-free way of doing anything. If a farmer were to decide to take a chance and plant a new and different crop—ragweed, for example, instead of the wheat that grew so well the previous year—it could lead to tragic dietary problems for the tribe or family.

That genetic predispositions to behavior can be leftover survival strategies from prehistoric times is a theme most recently echoed in a recent *Time* magazine cover story on the brain. It pointed out that the craving for fat among some people in parts of the world that experience periodic famine would ensure the survival of those who were able to store large quantities of this nutrient under their skin. "But the same tendencies cause mass heart failure when expressed in a fast-food world," the authors point out.

Even the genetic inclination to alcoholism may have positive prehistoric roots, according to evolutionists Randolph Nesse and George Williams in their book *Why We Get Sick.* The persistence of an alcoholic in the face of social, familial, and biological resistance and disaster, they say, reflects an evolutionary tenacity to go after neurochemical rewards despite obstacles. This tenacity may in some way be responsible for the continued growth, survival, and evolution of our species.

So the agricultural revolution highlighted two very different types of human societies: farmers and hunter/gatherers. They lived different lives, in different places. Those persons in farming societies with the ADD gene were probably culled out of the gene pool by natural selection, or they became warriors for their society, now hunting other humans as various tribes came into conflict. In some societies, evolving into the countries of Japan and India, this was even institutionalized into a caste system. History is replete with anecdotes about the unique personalities of the warrior castes such as the Kshatriya in India and the Samurai in Japan.

Where Have All the Hunters Gone?

If we accept for a moment the possibility that the gene that causes ADD was useful in another time and place but has become a liability in our modern, agriculture-derived industrial society, then the question arises: why isn't there more of it? How did we reach a point in human evolution where the farmers so massively outnumber the hunters? If the "hunting gene" was useful for the survival of people, why have hunting societies largely died out around the world? Why is ADD only seen among 3 to 20 percent of the population (depending on how you measure it and whose numbers you use), instead of 50 percent or some other number?

Recent research from several sources shows how hunting societies are *always* wiped out by farming societies over time. Fewer than 10 percent of hunting society members will normally survive when their culture collides with an agricultural society. And it has nothing to do with the hunter's "attention deficits," or with any inherent superiority of the farmers.

In one study reported in *Discover* magazine, the authors traced the root languages of the peoples living across central Africa. They found that at one time the area was dominated by hunter-gatherers: the Khoisans and the Pygmies. But over a period of several thousand years, virtually all of the Khoisans and Pygmies (the "Hottentots" and the "Bushmen" as they've been referred to in Western literature) were wiped out and replaced by Bantu-speaking farmers. Two entire groups of people were destroyed, rendering them nearly extinct, while the Bantu-speaking farmers flooded across the continent, dominating central Africa.

The reasons for this startling transformation are several.

First, agriculture is more efficient at generating calories than hunting. Because the same amount of land can support up to ten times more people when farming rather than hunting, farming societies generally have roughly ten times the population density of hunting societies. In war, numbers are always an advantage, particularly in these ratios. Few armies in history have survived an onslaught by another army ten times larger.

Second, diseases such as chicken pox, influenza, and measles, which have virtually wiped out vulnerable populations (such as native North and South Americans who died by the thousands when exposed to the diseases of the invading Europeans), began as diseases of domesticated animals. The farmers who were regularly exposed to such diseases developed relative immunities. While they would become ill, these germs usually wouldn't kill them. Those with no prior exposure and thus no immunity, however, would often die. So when farmers encountered hunters, they were killed off just by exposure to the Farmer's diseases.

And finally, agriculture provides physical stability to a culture. The tribe stays in one spot while their population grows. This provides them with time to specialize in individual jobs: some people become tool-and weapon-makers, others build devices which can be used in war, and others create governments, armies, and kingdoms. This gives farmers a huge technological advantage over hunting societies, which are generally more focused on day-to-day survival issues.

So now we have an answer to the question: "Where have all the hunters gone?"

Most were killed off, from Europe to Asia, from Africa to the Americas. Those who survived were brought into farming cultures either through assimilation, kidnapping, or cultural change, and provide the genetic material that appears in that small percentage of people with ADD.

Further evidence of the anthropological basis of ADD is seen among the modern survivors of ancient hunting societies.

Indigenous Hunters Today

Cultural anthropologist Jay Fikes, Ph.D., points out that members of traditional Native American hunting tribes behave, as a norm, differently from those who have traditionally been farmers. The farmers, such as the Hopi and other Pueblo Indian tribes, are relatively sedate and risk-averse, he says, whereas the hunters, such as the Navajo, are "constantly scanning their environment and more immediately sensitive to nuances. They're also the ultimate risk-takers. They and the Apaches were great raiders and warriors."

A physician who recently read my first book, and concluded that he saw proof of the Hunter/Farmer concept in his work with some of the Native Americans in Southwest Arizona, dropped me the following unsolicited note over the Internet:

"Many of these descendants of the Athabaskan Indians of Western Canada have never chosen to adapt to farming. They had no written language until an Anglo minister, fairly recently, wrote down their language for the first time. They talk 'heart to heart,' and there is little 'clutter' between you and them when you are communicating. They hear and consider everything you say. They are scanning all the time, both visually and auditorally. Time has no special meaning unless it is absolutely necessary (that's something we Anglos have imposed on them). They don't use small talk, but get right to the point, and have a deep understanding of people and the spiritual. And their history shows that they have a love of risk-taking."

Will Krynen, M.D., noted the same differences when he worked for the Canadian government as the doctor for several native North American tribes, and during the years he worked for the Red Cross as a physician in Southeast Asia. After reading my first book, he wrote:

"I've worked among indigenous hunting societies in many parts of the world, from Asia to the Americas. Over and over again I see among their adults and children that constellation of behaviors we call ADD. In those societies, however, these behaviors are highly adaptive and actually contribute to the societies' success.

"Among the members of the tribes of northern Canada, such as the caribou hunters of the McKenzie Basin, these adaptive characteristics—constantly scanning their environment, quick decision-making (impulsiveness), and a willingness to take risks—contribute every year to the tribe's survival.

"These same behaviors, however, often make it difficult for tribal children to succeed in western schools when we try to impose our western curriculum on them."

But what sent humankind onto the radical social departure from hunting to farming? Few other animals, with the exception of highly organized insects such as ants, have developed a society that is based on anything that approaches agriculture.

In *The Ascent of Man*, Jacob Bronowski points out that 20,000 years ago every human on earth was a hunter and forager. The most advanced hunting societies had started following wild herd animals, as is still done by modern Laplanders. This had been the basis of human and pre-human society and lifestyle for several million years.

Until 1995, the earliest hard evidence of human activity (and hunting activity at that) came from the Olduvai Gorge in Tanzania, Africa, with fragments of stone tools and weapons that dated back 2.5 million years. More recently, University of Southern California anthropologist Craig Stanford is quoted in the *Chicago Tribune* as saying that recent research he conducted in Africa indicates that early hominids may have been tribally hunting as early as 6 million years ago.

So for 6 million years we and our ancestors were hunters, and suddenly, in a tiny moment of time (10,000 years is to 6 million as less than 3 minutes is to a 24-hour day) the entire human race veered in a totally new direction.

The Agricultural Revolution

The reason for the change, according to Bronowski and many anthropologists, probably has to do with the end of the last ice age, which roughly corresponds to the beginning of the agricultural revolution. (Bronowski and most authorities place the agricultural revolution as occurring roughly 12,000 years ago.) At that time, mutated grasses appeared simultaneously on several continents, probably in response to the sudden and radical change in climate. These grasses were the first high-yield, edible ancestors of modern rice and wheat, and provided the humans who lived near where they appeared with an opportunity to nurture and grow these staple foods.

Those people with the Farmer-like patience to grow the crops evolved into the farming societies, and ridded their ranks of the impulsive, sensation-seeking Hunters among them. Those persons who were not patient enough to wait for rice to grow maintained their hunting tribes, the last remnants of which we see today in a few remaining indigenous peoples on the earth. The Old Testament, for example, is in large part the story of a nomadic hunting tribe moving through the wrenching process, over several generations, of becoming a settled farming tribe.

Eastern Religious Views of ADD

In India there also appears to be a very different view of ADD than is conventional in the United States. During the monsoon season of 1993, the week of the Hyderabad earthquake, I took a 12-hour train ride halfway across the subcontinent to visit an obscure town near the Bay of Bengal. In the train compartment with me were several Indian businessmen and a physician; we had plenty of time to talk as the countryside flew by from sunrise to sunset.

Curious about how they viewed ADD, I said, "Are you familiar with the personality type where people seem to crave stimulation but have a hard time staying with any one thing? They hop from career to career, and sometimes even from relationship to relationship, and never seem to settle down."

"Ah, we know this type well," one of the men said, the other two nodding in agreement.

"What do you call it?" I asked.

"Very holy," he said. "These are old souls, near the end of their karmic cycle." Again the other three nodded agreement, perhaps a bit more vigorously in response to my startled look.

"Old souls?" I said, thinking that a very odd description for what we call a disorder.

"Yes," the physician said, taking his turn in the conversation. "In our religion, we believe that the purpose of reincarnation is to eventually free oneself from worldly entanglement and desire. In each lifetime we experience certain lessons, until finally we are free of this earth and can merge into the oneness of what you would call God. When a soul is very close to the end of those thousands of incarnations, he must take a few lifetimes and do many, many things, to clean up the little threads left over from his previous lifetimes."

"This is a man very close to becoming enlightened," the first businessman added. "We have great respect for such individuals, although their lives may be difficult."

Another of the businessmen raised a finger and interjected: "But it is the difficulties of such lives that purify the soul." The others nodded agreement.

"In America we consider this a psychiatric disorder," I said. All three looked startled, then laughed.

"In America, you consider our most holy men, our yogis and swamis, to be crazy people, too," said the physician with a touch of sadness in his voice. "So it is with different cultures. We live in different worlds."

In the Hunter/warrior societies of northern India and Europe, religious rituals were developed to teach focusing and concentration. These include saying the Rosary in the Roman Catholic tradition, with the beads serving to provide a form of biofeedback, constantly reminding the person not to allow their mind to wander. In Hinduism prayer beads called a Mala are often used in Mantra meditation, where a single sound (such as "Om") is repeated over and over again.

That the Hunting societies, with their culturally-ingrained prevalence of ADD-like behaviors and highly distractible people, would create concentrative religious rituals to teach them to focus makes perfect sense. Focusing is something which doesn't come naturally to their people, so it's evolved as a learned behavior in the culture.

In traditionally agricultural societies, however, the meditative techniques are quite different.

From Trungpa Rimpoche and Ösel Tensig I learned Vipassana, or mindfulness, and practiced the technique for ten to fifteen hours a day at Karme Chöling. In this Tibetan Buddhist system, the goal is not to concentrate the mind on one point, but to empty the mind and be fully aware. It's practiced with the eyes open; whenever a thought arises which may become the focus of concentration, we visualized it as a bubble we would mentally reach out and pop as we noted to ourselves that we were thinking. This released the thought and returned the mind to empty awareness.

The goal of this form of meditation is not focus, but its opposite. As Berkeley-based Chilean psychiatrist Claudio Naranjo wrote in his essay, *On the Psychology of Meditation*, Vipassana and Zen represent "the negative way" form of meditation, and come from the East. Mantra, rosary, mandala, and prayer represent the opposite, Western "concentrative or absorptive meditation."

Thus, the agricultural societies of southern Asia, farmers for millennia with a highly focused society and people, naturally developed cultural rituals which train awareness and distractibility. These systems teach them to resist their natural impulse to concentrate their attention.

Shunryu Suzuki (1905-1971), one of Japan's most famous Zen masters, founded the Zen Center in San Francisco, which I visited briefly in the late 1960s. In the prologue to *Zen Mind, Beginner's Mind*, a collection of his talks, he writes:

"In Japan we have the phrase *shoshin*, which means 'beginner's mind.' The goal of [Zen] practice is always to keep our beginner's mind...."

That in the West we have missed this distinction between types of religious rituals and their significance when viewing context-or spectrum-disorders like ADD is largely attributable to the influence of Sigmund Freud on modern psychological and philosophical thought. He wrote forcefully against religion and its seductions, noting that "the derivation of religious needs [come] from the infant's helplessness and the longing for the father." Carl Jung was the first psychologist of any stature to challenge Freud's view and assert that meditative practice wasn't itself an expression of neurosis, but perhaps even a potential treatment for illness. Erich Fromm later developed these ideas even more fully, but Fromm and Jung are still both largely outside the mainstream of contemporary psychotherapeutic thought.

A view ranging from world history to entrepreneurship to religion and culture amply shows the distinctions between Hunters and Farmers. And we see that the institutions of contemporary Western society, rooted as they are in the agricultural/industrial model, tend to make misfits of Hunters.

Solutions

Whether or not the Hunter/Farmer model as a way of viewing ADD is ultimately demonstrated to be good science may be less than vital. For the moment, it provides us with a way to view this condition that leaves self-esteem intact. It accurately models and predicts how and why medications are helpful, and reframes our techniques for working with Hunter-type individuals in schools, the work place, and in relationships.

Like the (as yet unproved) electron-flow model for explaining electricity, the Hunter/Farmer paradigm allows us to get our hands around a phenomenon, wield it to our benefit, and empower the lives of people.

If ADD is part of our genetic heritage, it cannot be seen as an excuse for a person's failings. It's merely an explanation of behavior, one that then provides the first steps toward overcoming those obstacles which, in the past, so often caused failure.

Nonetheless, we can try to reform our schools, in particular, to make them more Hunter-friendly. This would include having more active instructional methods, more hands-on work for children, shorter class times, smaller class sizes, and exercise between classes whenever possible.

What Maslow Overlooked:
The Need to Feel Alive

"People say that what we're all seeking is a meaning for life. I don't think that's what we're really seeking. I think that what we're seeking is an experience of being alive, so that our life experiences on the purely physical plane will have resonances within our own innermost being and reality, so that we actually feel the rapture of being alive."
—Joseph Campbell, *The Power of Myth* (1988)

When Abraham Maslow wrote *Motivation and Personality* back in 1954, he didn't have the advantage we do now of a reasonably thorough knowledge of neurochemistry. He observed people and the way they interacted with the world, and developed his theory of the "hierarchy of human needs," which ranged from the need for safety to the need for social interaction to the need for what some may call religious experience.

But Maslow had his own particular neurochemistry, which colored his observations and caused him to overlook a critical point. This overlooked basic human need may, in fact, be so critical to an understanding of human nature that understanding it gives us a revelatory flash of insight into the nature of personality disorders and specifically attention deficit disorder (ADD). This is what I call "the need to feel aliveness," and it also explains why some people have multiple jobs, mates, and lifestyles, whereas others settle into one fixed routine and stay with it their entire lives, apparently quite happy in their stasis.

To understand how Maslow could have overlooked a fundamental human need which drives the behaviors of as much as 30% of our population, it's important to first understand how a particular part of our brain is wired. This part of the brain, and the way it works, can cause this need to come into being, or, to remain unexpressed.

The part of the brain which most likely drives this process is called the thalamus.

Our sensory volume control

All of our senses except smell flow into a small structure near the base of the brain called the thalamus. When we hear, see, feel, or taste something, that information from the sensory organs and nerves is first passed along to the thalamus, before being relayed to the rest of the brain.

What our eyes see, for example, moves along as electrochemical impulses through the optic nerves (through the optic chiasma) to a part of the thalamus dedicated to vision. From there, the signals project to the part of our brain that actually sees, the primary visual cortex located in the occipital lobe of the cerebral cortex. The same process occurs with sound, smell, and taste.

The thalamus acts in much the same way as a faucet does on a sink. Sensory inputs pass through it on the way to their final destination (much like water must pass through a faucet to reach the sink). The faucet of the thalamus controls how much of that information reaches its ultimate destination—and how quickly and at what level of strength.

Another model, suggested by Dr. Dale Hammerschmidt of the University of Minnesota's Medical School, is of the thalamus as a graphic equalizer on a stereo system. This is probably a more accurate way of looking at it, as the thalamus doesn't apply the same amplification or attenuation to each sense. Some people are more sensitive to sight, others to hearing, others to touch, and some to taste, or any combination of these four. These anomalies are sometimes the result of thalamic variations. However, I'll use the faucet metaphor here both because of its simplicity and because not everyone is familiar with a graphic equalizer.

Another important brain structure connected with the

thalamus is the reticular formation (often called the Reticular Activating System or RAS).

The RAS is a large group of nerve cells which originate deep within the brain. Long nerve cells that look like fibers grow up from this area through the thalamus, and then extend on out into and throughout various parts of the cortex (our thinking brain). It's as if the thalamus had a little curled-up porcupine underneath it, with disproportionately long quills which stick up into virtually every important part of the conscious brain.

Largely on orders from the thalamus, the RAS tells the conscious brain how alert it should be. The RAS is responsible for the startle reflex, and is one of the primary control systems for our general level of arousal or awakeness.

The thalamus and the RAS are the ever-vigilant doorkeepers of our senses, and, as part of our most ancient brain structures, they have as a primary responsibility to provide information to the brain for that most ancient of instincts—the fight-or-flight response. They are responsible for our safety and survival (at the most primal level of Maslow's hierarchy).

Let us say that the thalamus gets an unusual input from the eyes or ears—say a loud noise or the sight of something flying at us. Instead of just normally passing it along to the cortex so we could think about it, the thalamus will do two things:

First, it turns up the volume level for that particular sight or sound, so our conscious brain will notice it more vividly. (People who've been in car accidents often relate how clearly they remember seeing the oncoming car, for example. This is the result, in part, of the thalamus having opened up the faucet, thus producing a more memorable impression on the brain.)

Second, the thalamus will activate the RAS, saying, "Hey, wake up the rest of the brain! Something important and maybe dangerous is happening out there!" The very long and super-efficient nerves of the RAS transmit a whoops!/startle impulse to the brain, that adds a huge dose of impact to our sight, sound, feeling, or taste.

The RAS and thalamus are so powerfully involved in maintaining and modulating our level of awareness or awakeness, that if either are accidentally damaged during surgery or in an accident the person will slip into a permanent coma. Similarly, it is believed that when someone sustains a concussion which knocks them unconscious, it's because the RAS has been jarred hard enough to shut itself down as a defense strategy.

So, in combination, our thalamus and our RAS control how much of the world around us we sense—how fast and with what volume the input flows through the faucet of the thalamus, and how awake or aware we are as we process that input.

People with a wide-open thalamic faucet are awash in sensory input.

Closed and Open Faucets

One of the more interesting recent medical discoveries is the fact that each one of us has a slightly different "normal" setting for how open or closed the faucet of our thalamus is, and also how hair-triggered our RAS may be at activating the rest of the brain.

People with a wide-open thalamic faucet experience sight, sound, touch, and taste as being strong and vivid: they're flooded with sensory input. The result is that they often want to back away from the world. Their sensory experience is sometimes painfully bright. Boisterous conversation or loud music overloads their brains, and they're uncomfortable with strong touch or other intense physical sensation.

These people are sometimes referred to as introverts, although in the context of Carl Jung's original meaning for the term this is a misnomer. Nonetheless, people with a very active thalamus and RAS tend to be quiet, withdrawn, and to dislike wild disruptions in their lives. Their primary life strategy is often avoidance of excess sensation, pain, emotion, or disruption.

So much input is flowing through the thalamus and RAS into the cortex that they necessarily step back from life and look for a little peace and quiet.

On the other end of the spectrum are those people whose thalamus and RAS are not as open: less sensory information flows through, or flows through with a lower intensity. People with a more-closed thalamic faucet experience the world as "too quiet."

Since the faucet is closed a bit tighter, less continuous sensory stimulation comes through, and it takes a much more dramatic event to punch through and activate their reticular startle response.

These people see, hear, taste, and feel (in terms of sensation, not emotion) less vividly. Rather than trying to push themselves away from the world, they throw themselves into it, often with an intensity that is bewildering to the open-faucet-thalamus folks.

Since it takes a stronger sensory input to make it through the faucet of their thalamus and RAS and into their thinking/experiencing brain (the cortex), these people are not overwhelmed by bright lights, strong colors, loud sounds, intense physical sensations, or strong tastes. If anything, they enjoy these things, because such sensations bring them, if only for a few moments, into a more close and intimate contact with a world they may normally feel is a bit distant.

We've all known people who fit into the two extreme ends of this spectrum: they're stereotypes or clichés in our society and in popular literature.

Closed-faucet folks who crave stimulation live for the party, love to perform in front of people, are enthusiastic about skydiving or roller coasters, and consume hot peppers with an enthusiasm that baffles their friends.

Open-faucet folks, inundated by sensory input, just want to be left alone, don't generally speak up, appreciate subtle things such as fine art and classical music, and often are quick to dismiss the closed-faucet folks as boors or egomaniacs.

And then, of course, there are those people who fall in the middle between these two extremes. The world is vivid to them, but not painful. They have enough sensory input to satisfy them, so they don't go out of their way to create more for themselves, yet they're not so overpowered by it that they feel the need to withdraw. These people are the ones who some would consider "normal," and Woody Guthrie loved to write and sing songs about them , e.g., "Little Boxes."

But what, you may ask, does this have to do with basic human needs and things like ADD?

A Human Basic Need: To Experience Our Own "Aliveness"

Psychologist Abraham Maslow gave us a remarkable look into human behavior when he outlined his hierarchy of needs. Maslow pointed out that, "The human being is a wanting animal and rarely reaches a state of complete satisfaction except for a short time."

Similarly, one of the basic tenants of Buddhist thought is that humans are always wanting something. Buddha's four noble truths are: (1) All life is suffering. (2) The cause of suffering is desire. (3) Give up desire and you end suffering. (4) The eight-fold path to end desire (right thought, action, livelihood, remembrance, meditation, belief, speech, and exertion).

This is such a basic and universal tenant of human nature that we find it in virtually all philosophies and religions. Jesus said, "Lay not up your treasures where moth and rust doth corrupt." Rabbi Isaac Luria, the Ari, also known as the Lion of Safed and one of the most famous of the 16th century scholars and mystics of Kabbalah, wrote in what was later translated as *Ten Luminous Emanations* about the importance of separating self from the desire for experience. In Hinduism, part of the Bodhisattva vow is to give up even the desire to give up desire. And, of course, Freud, Adler, Skinner, and other psychologists have pointed out that many of those behaviors we define as neurotic are really misdirected attempts to satisfy basic needs, or are the result of unfulfilled basic needs.

Maslow wrote that our most basic need is for biological stasis. We need water, food, appropriate nutrition, to excrete, and to maintain our body at a constant temperature.

The second level he identified as the need for safety.

Once these basic physical needs are met, then we go off in search of our third need, which he identified as the need for love and belonging. When that's met, we'll start seeking self-esteem and status. And, finally, when all these physical and emotional needs are satisfied, a person will turn to what some might call spiritual needs, and which Maslow called the need for self-actualization.

Maslow's insight into this hierarchy or pyramid of needs had a revolutionary impact on the field of psychology, creating a whole new school of psychological thought called Humanistic Psychology, and was profoundly insightful. He shows us why a person who is starving will not care much about his social status. For example, in 1980 in northern Uganda I went into a famine area to help set up a feeding center and hospital for starving refugees. Not only did they not worry about their appearance, many didn't even care if they were wearing clothes.

Maslow points out some misconceptions many people have: for example, what we describe in western society as hunger, he calls appetite. Few of us have ever experienced life-threatening hunger, which is at the foundation of the pyramid of needs, or even when we say we are hungry, most of the time we simply crave a specific taste or flavor, or want that pleasant feeling of fullness in our stomach. This isn't a stasis or survival need, but more likely a self-esteem or some other higher need.

Extending this concept, I believe that an understanding of the thalamus and RAS, and the study of ADD, have revealed to us a basic human need that Maslow didn't include in his hierarchy. I define this as "The need to experience aliveness: the need to feel that one is alive."

Cogito, ergo sum, the philosopher René Descartes wrote in 1637, which means *I think, therefore I am.* Yet merely thinking is not enough to create, in many people, the reality—the down-in-the-gut knowledge—that *therefore I am.*

To validate *therefore I am,* we must experience the fact of our aliveness. Ugo Betti wrote: "At any given moment I open my eyes and exist. And before that, during all eternity, what was there? Nothing."

We see that in different people, different thresholds of sensation are necessary in order to experience gratification of this basic human need to feel alive.

Nobel-prize-winning poet, playwright, author and philosopher Rabindranath Tagore, for example, had a life devoted to quiet meditation and contemplation. He enjoyed sitting quietly and pondering the nature of things, living within his mind (so to speak), presumably because his need for sensory input was adequately satisfied. The faucet of his thalamus and RAS was probably wide open, and life came in at him full-force. The writings he left us say things such as, "That I exist is a perpetual surprise which is life." Similar descriptions of the naturalness of aliveness, the fulfillment of that "need to experience aliveness" simply from being alive, can be found in the writings of many others, from Thomas Merton to George Santayana.

These people had their "need to feel alive" satisfied from birth. Their thalamus and RAS were open wide enough to experience the world constantly, in full Technicolor. Like a person after a perpetual Thanksgiving dinner they felt full all their lives.

Those with a thalamic faucet that's more closed, however, need to periodically leap up through the baseline set by their thalamus to gasp in a full breath of aliveness. Their lives are characterized by a constant search for stimulation, and many are tortured by this basic need to feel alive on a daily basis.

The philosopher Pascal wrote in 1670, "There is a pleasure in being in a ship beaten about by a storm, when we are sure that it will not founder." Would Tagore have said the same? Probably not. Pascal would have probably enjoyed The Scream Machine roller coaster at the famous Six Flags Over Georgia amusement park; Tagore would have probably dismissed it as crude and overly stimulating.

So we have here now a final "basic human need," one which Freud first came close to nailing down in 1933 when he wrote about the Id: "We can come nearer to the Id with images, and call it a chaos, a cauldron of seething excitement.... These instincts fill it with energy, but it has no organization and no unified will, only an impulsion to obtain satisfaction for the instinctual needs, in accordance with the pleasure principle."

This is not to say that the basic human need to experience "aliveness" is the same as what Freud called the Id, but I do believe that Freud was close to touching this need when he embarked on an exploration of those driving and motivating forces which lie below our normal levels of waking consciousness. After all, consider how few people are sufficiently self-aware to say, for example, "I like to drive fast because it makes me feel more alive."

Yet how else to explain this sort of behavior, unless we leap to the conclusion (as Freud and others sometimes have) that such behavior must demonstrate an unconscious death wish? The idea of an unconscious death wish is interesting and, no doubt, occasionally true, but it doesn't explain the liking of spicy foods, loud music, vivid colors, wild sex, and other types of sensation-seeking behavior that are often associated with the types of people who also drive like maniacs. They can't *all* be trying to kill themselves!

So if these folks aren't trying to kill themselves with all this sensation-seeking, what is their goal?

Perhaps it's a Life Wish: *To wake up, even if just for an instant a day, and viscerally know that they are alive.*

Characterizing this previously-undefined human need as the basis of these behaviors then gives us a whole new key to understand both healthy high-stimulation activities as well as destructive and self-destructive stimulation-seeking behaviors. In both cases, the person seeks the experience of aliveness. In the former, they've found appropriate ways to get it (skydiving, public speaking, sales, politics, substitute teaching, being an emergency room physician). In the latter case they've stumbled into—often by life circumstances which shut out the appropriate routes—destructive ways to experience stimulation (mugging people, taking drugs, having frequent sex with a wide variety of people, starting fights, gambling).

And how does this help us better understand ADD and other variations from the norm?

ADD and Trout

Anybody who's ever gone fly-fishing is familiar with the behavior of those fish who eat insects off the surface of the water. The pond or stream is perfectly still, then the surface is disturbed as a small bug touches the water, trapped because its wings become wet. A small ripple emanates from the insect, as it struggles to use surface tension as a lever to free and dry a wing. Suddenly the water's surface is shattered as a fish comes surging up from below, snaps the bug and a big gulp of air into its open mouth, and then crashes back through the surface to vanish into the water's depths.

Similarly, people with ADD often appear hyperactive because they're periodically leaping up through the surface of stimulus—a surface defined by the set-point of their thalamus and RAS— to try to grab a little bit of aliveness.

For example, little Howie is sitting in class while the teacher is droning on about long division, a subject which Howie either has already mastered or doesn't care about. Howie's thalamus and RAS aren't letting much information in, and the world is starting to seem rather gray and distant. The thinking cortex, the *therefore, I am* part of his brain, is gasping for air and wants to leap at that bug: "Give me sensation," it's saying, "so I'll know that I'm still alive."

The urge is overwhelming: a basic human need is unfulfilled. Something has to happen. The brain is screaming: "Break through the surface!"

So Howie leans forward and pulls Sally's pony tail, or lets out a loud burp, or flips a spitball at Billy. Bang! The classroom erupts and now the world is back in vivid color.

This simple action has penetrated the thin membranous surface of sensation that, like the pond's surface, the thalamus had inserted between Howie's mind and his experience of the world.

As an adult, Howie may tell an off-color joke, or cut someone off in traffic, or start his own business—anything to propel the brain up through the surface to gasp that breath (or snatch that bug) of aliveness.

If we look at the three basic behaviors associated with ADD, for example, we can reframe each of them in this context. They are: distractibility, impulsivity, and sensation-seeking or risk-taking. ADD-H (hyperactive) adds the fourth behavior of hyperactivity, illustrated by little Howie at school.

Howie's Distractibility

The scanning behavior of distractibility, viewed in this light, is the brain's way of opening itself up to the experience of aliveness.

The boring teacher is droning on and on, and little Howie has already become distractible, looking around to see that Sally is very concerned with how neatly her pony tail is brushed, that

Billy is carefully listening to the teacher, and that no one else is paying attention to him.

If he's learned some physical self-control and has an active imagination, Howie may drift off into daydreaming instead of acting out, creating a vivid internal world that stimulates him. The Calvin and Hobbes cartoons virtually define this behavior. We see Calvin's internal world for several panels, then have that world shattered as Calvin is brought back to reality by Miss Wormwood standing over him with a ruler asking him to answer the question. Similarly, psychiatrist John Ratey of the Harvard Medical School points out that girls more often fit into this category of "internal distractibility" than do boys, both because of social conditioning and because of actual differences in male and female brains.

But whether Howie drifts into daydreaming, or moves into action, he starts out with distractibility: his brain is seeking out new sources of incoming sensory information in order to wake it back up.

Impulsivity

Since we're dealing here with a basic human need, all the scholarly and erudite attempts to explain ADD as having to do with defects in cognitive processes, disinhibition, or the frontal lobes (among others) really become secondary, if not outright irrelevant.

A truly hungry person will grab for food, often regardless of the consequences, as I learned in 1980. When my companion and I opened the trunk of the car we'd used to bring supplies from Kenya into the old Namalu Prison Farm (then turned into a refugee center) I was nearly trampled in the stampede of pre-viously-docile teenagers and old women. People barely able to move because of disease or malnutrition were suddenly scream-ing, kicking, biting, and climbing over each other.

Just as the unmet basic human need for biological stasis (food, in this example) will drive people to otherwise unthinkable behaviors, so too will the basic human need to experience alive-ness when it's not met.

The brain is yelling, "Now, now, I need it *now* to be sure I'm still alive," and it's small wonder that Howie doesn't take the time to consider the long-term consequences of cutting a loud fart. Or that Johnny and Sue don't stop their progressively intense kissing to drive down to the drugstore for a condom. Or that Ralph tells his boss what he really thinks of him. Or that Bill leans over and tells Ruth what he heard about Ruth's husband and that woman down in accounting.

Get a reaction. Get a response. Shake up the world. Make a decision and act—NOW. *Wake up!*

Restlessness or Risk-Taking

While most authorities cite the third primary symptom of ADD as restlessness, many are now including risk-taking, or "the restive search for high stimulation."

In this context, however, the conventional symptom of rest-lessness is actually just stimulation-seeking—and risk-taking also fills precisely the same need. In fact if you combine stimulation-seeking with impulsivity, what you get is a virtually perfect defini-tion of risk-taking.

The equation here is simple: the more risk, the more adrenaline. And, as you may have guessed, adrenaline and its close relatives are the neurotransmitters to which the thalamus and RAS are most sensitive.

Some of us look at those people who are perpetual risk-takers and shake our heads in amazement. How could Bill Clinton have put up with all that abuse in the primaries and during the election campaign, particularly after being accused of marital infidelity and drug-use which had so recently sunk the presidential aspira-tion of Gary Hart and the Supreme Court aspiration of Judge Ginsberg? How could Lewis and Clark have persisted in their long voyage to map the interior of this wild nation despite hostile natives, disease, wild animals, and the combined threats of winter and starvation? How could the early settlers of America been willing to take the boat ride across the Atlantic in the 16th and 17th centuries when, on average, ten percent of the people who left Europe died during the trip here? How could a nurse or physician continue to work in an emergency room when every day, every hour, it's one crisis after another? Or a police officer risk his life on the streets? Or a combat pilot engage in dangerous missions? How could someone engage in an extramarital affair, or in unprotected sex? How can anyone eat that lethally hot chili?

The answer, of course, is that people do these things because it satisfies a basic need in them. The experience of taking chances jolts them with sensation, and thus wakes up in them that feeling of aliveness—a need more basic and visceral than virtually any other except biological stasis. As author André Gide wrote in his *Journals* in 1924, "It is only in adventure that some people succeed in knowing themselves, in finding themselves."

This also explains why a compulsive gambler, a sexually promiscuous person, or a compulsive criminal will often continue to take those same risks, even when they experience the negative consequences of them. The entrepreneur and the break-in artist are running off the same brain biochemistry.

"Everything is sweetened by risk," said Alexander Smith (1830-1867), the famous 19th century author of Dreamthorp (1883) and other works. And John F. Kennedy, who took the nuclear-annihilation risk of staring down Kruschev during the Cuban Missile Crisis, and the risk of sleeping with a variety of women during his presidency, said in a 1961 speech, "Any danger spot is tenable if men—brave men—will make it so."

The "Paradoxical Effect" Explained

It's been known for years that if you give stimulant drugs to hyperactive kids, they settle down. But no textbook on pharmacology or psychiatry can tell you why. Therefore, this oddity has been referred to in the literature as the "paradoxical effect."

But, if this thalamic/RAS model is correct, the hyperactive kids are the ones whose brains are the most starved for stimulation. Their thalamus and RAS are closed down more than the average person, thus letting less stimulus into their brains. Their brains are begging to be awakened, to be stimulated, and so they incite stimulation by jumping out of the chair or speaking out of turn. They have a basic human need which is not being met by the boring classrooms or comfortable life of modern society.

Stimulant drugs, from Ritalin to amphetamine to caffeine to cocaine, open the faucet of the thalamus. They make the RAS more active, and more aggressive in sending wake-up signals to the cortex. In other words, to use the fish jumping out the water example—they lift the person's consciousness *above* the water level, into a place where it's constantly bright and interesting. The person then no longer experiences the need to leap up and crash through the surface.

Now that his basic human need of aliveness is satisfied, little Howie doesn't need to scan his environment for interesting things. He's no longer distractible, because the level of light, sound, touch, and taste around him have all jumped up a notch or two. This increasing flow of stimulus satisfies his need to experience aliveness, and, now that this basic need is met, he can sit quietly in the chair and attend to the teacher's instructions.

Similarly, when medicated with stimulants, he's not feeling that underlying drivenness that comes from having a basic human need unfulfilled. Because he's not feeling driven to fill a need any longer, it's easy for him now to toss thoughts over to the frontal lobes for deliberate and careful consideration. He need no longer be impulsive. Thinking things through is not boring any more, simply because Howie himself—his baseline, his *therefore, I am* is no longer experiencing an unfilled need. In other words, *Howie* is no longer bored, so things around him cease to be boring.

Howie is now less likely to engage in risk-taking such as grabbing Sally's pony tail, because he now has enough sensation in his world. He'll soon discover, when medicated, if he does things to increase his sensation level, he'll experience discomfort, perhaps even panic. Those things that used to make him feel good, that once fulfilled his need for aliveness, now overwhelm him. And so he stops the risk-taking and settles down into becoming a "normal" citizen of his school or family or world.

This view of ADD also explains behavior like procrastination and overcommitment: both are simply ways of creating a crisis, thus bringing up the adrenaline levels so the sense of aliveness is more acute.

ADD Manifestations

In placing the "need to experience aliveness" on Maslow's scale of human needs, we see a variety of ways in which people can fulfill this need. Maslow points out that people are rarely stuck in just one of the levels of the hierarchy, but operate instead at different levels simultaneously. We tend to have one primary place where we're dealing with life's issues at any given moment in time. For a closed-faucet person, that place will always be colored by a need to feel aliveness, because this need is so primal.

It may be that we're mostly struggling with the need for a place to live, or perhaps that the need to be loved is primary in our lives. Or even the need for self-actualization drives us as Maslow said it did him.

When we know whether a person is closed-or open-faucet, we can predict how they'll express or act out their other needs. Closed-faucet people struggling with the need for love will be distracted by the opposite sex, make impulsive decisions about relationships, and take risky chances in those relationships. Those people struggling with the need for self-actualization, on the other hand, will leap from group to group, guru to guru, in the quest for new experience and insight. Of course, you could apply this logic to any level of need and behavior.

Open-faucet people, on the other hand, will be more cautious in their seeking and less likely to connect with high-stim situations, people, or relationships.

When I shared this concept of a new basic human need that Maslow may have overlooked with psychotherapist George Lynn, he observed: "Your emphasis on this additional human need to feel alive in Maslow's Hierarchy makes a lot of sense. This explains the rage that my ADD clients' parents tell me their kids experience in school. *Rage may be a response to having a basic need suffocated or starved.*" (Italics added.)

This is so common-sensible as to be intuitive, particularly for those people with a closed-faucet thalamus/RAS who have experienced this in their own lives. These kids and adults *are* different from the norm, and their core self will instinctively resist being squashed into society's proverbial round hole.

Is it Learned or Built-in?

This discussion of distractibility, impulsivity, and risk-taking in the context of the set-point of the thalamus and RAS may cause one to conclude that these behaviors are hard-wired into our brains, and therefore unchangeable with anything short of a drug or surgery which would reset the thalamus.

A careful look, though, will suggest otherwise. The thalamic set-point creates conditions in which particular behaviors are most easily learned, but is not in and of itself responsible for those behaviors.

For example, if a baby with a closed-faucet thalamus is feeling the need for more input, he or she may start to look around the room in search of stimulus. This distractible behavior is rewarded when the baby sees the mobile over her bed, and the first step toward learning how to behave distractedly is formed in the young brain.

Similarly, if the baby is feeling the need for stimulation and impulsively reaches out and grabs a vase, shattering it on the floor, the reaction from mom (assuming it's not too negative) and the sensation of the sound and appearance of the shattering vase all teach her that impulsive grabbing produces sensation, which equals reward. And the risk-taking of crawling into new areas, poking the cat, pulling on the tablecloth, etc., all produce more and more interesting stimuli, which reaffirm to the child that he is alive—thus fulfilling that basic need.

On the other hand, a child born with a high thalamic set-point, a wide-open faucet, may be content to simply lay in his crib and play with his fingers. That soft sensation is enough to fill his cortex with input, to affirm his aliveness, and he doesn't then learn to behave in ways that we'd describe as distractible, impulsive, or risk-taking. If anything he'd learn the opposite lesson: the crash of the vase that would delight the low-stim baby by arousing his brain would represent an overwhelming and unpleasant amount of input for the baby with a high-stim setting on his thalamus and RAS.

We see that the behaviors most often associated with ADD are actually *learned* ways of fulfilling a basic need, but they're more-or-less-easily learned based on inherited brain chemistry and structure. The needs for these brain-structure differences, these different thalamic set-points, could reasonably be traced back to types of neurochemistry most useful in hunting or farming societies.

That this is both a function of the neurological set-point and of learned ways to satisfy the basic human need it mediates is clearly demonstrated by a twin study done in 1989 by Goodman and Stevenson. This study looked for symptoms of hyperactivity among 127 pairs of identical twins, and 111 pairs of fraternal twins. If what we call hyperactivity were purely biological with no learned component, one would expect to find a 100% concordance among the identical twins. If it was merely learned, it would probably be in the range found among the general population with a slight boost from the shared environment.

What they found was that among fraternal twins where one of the twins had been diagnosed as being hyperactive, the incidence of both twins being hyperactive was 33%. Among the identical twins, however, it jumped up to 51%. So clearly, even something as apparently baseline as hyperactivity contains both a nature and a nurture aspect.

Since these behaviors contain a learned component, it's reasonable to theorize that it should be possible to learn new, different, and more appropriate ways to fulfill needs, as did Abraham Maslow himself.

Why Maslow Overlooked this Need

In the last interview done with Abraham Maslow before he died in 1968, *Psychology Today* writer Mary Harrington Hall asked him about his own life and personality. He proudly spoke of how his father had hitchhiked all the way across Europe from Russia to arrive in America at the age of 15. And how he, himself, had dropped out of law school in his first year because, rather than studying one single topic, he wanted to study "everything."

In a reprint of that interview in 1992, *Psychology Today* author Edward Hoffman noted that Maslow was "temperamentally restless and ceaselessly active," and that he found convalescence at home from a major heart attack to be "almost painfully unbearable."

When asked by Hall, "How would you describe yourself? Who are you?" Maslow responded: "I'm someone who likes plowing new ground, then walking away from it. I get bored easily. For me, the big thrill comes with the discovering."

It would seem, then, that perhaps Abraham Maslow himself was a relatively closed-faucet person. He eagerly described in the interview moments from his life when he reached out for sensation, acted impulsively, and took risks. Some might say that his putting forth audacious new theories of human nature was, in itself, a highly risky activity.

Yet we're often blindest to our own nature. Without the context that the then-emerging field of neuropsychiatry could provide for his hierarchy of human needs, it would be easy for Maslow to assume that his own drivenness was merely a quest for satisfaction of the basic needs, or the cognitive needs (esthetic needs, and the desire to know and to understand) of self-actualization.

He acknowledged his tendency to overlook fundamental issues while buried in new work when he discussed his early research into sex. He'd studied the issue of human sexuality extensively for several years and was considered by many as an expert in the field. Reflecting on this time, he said in the *Psychology Today* interview: "One day, it suddenly dawned on me that I knew as much about sex as any man living—in the intellectual sense. I knew everything that had been written; I had made discoveries with which I was pleased; I had done therapeutic work. This was about ten years before the Kinsey report came out. Then I suddenly burst into laughter. Here was I, the great sexologist, and I had never seen an erect penis except one, and that was from my own bird's-eye view. That humbled me considerably."

The other reason Maslow omitted the need to feel aliveness in his hierarchy was that his most passionate life studies were of what he called "self-actualized" people. These men and women, who represent a fraction of one percent of the population, were those who had converted their drivenness through the various levels of human needs all the way up to the need for self-actualization. As such, they weren't what most psychologists would consider dysfunctional.

Yet it's in the study of dysfunctional people—those in prisons, or those who are failing in schools, or who can't keep a job or marriage together for more than a few months at a time—that we find the basic human need to experience aliveness most vividly painted.

Because these people never learned to express their need in higher ways, to transmute the energy of this need into the search for new chemicals or new theories of psychology or new lands, they demonstrate it in the rawest and most primal form. Maslow never looked at these kinds of people, even though they constitute a hugely larger population than his self-actualizers. Therefore it's not only understandable that Maslow would overlook this basic human need, it's predictable.

Solutions

Realizing that ADD children and adults are being driven not by an urge to be bad, but rather by an inborn and unmet basic human need, we can view their plight with more compassion and understanding.

We can also look to ways to build more stimulation and variety into their lives, be it in the classroom, the work place, at home or in relationships.

ADD As Hypervigilance Run Amok

"Man can preserve a vestige of spiritual freedom, of independence of mind, even in such terrible conditions of psychic and physical stress."
— Viktor Frankl, *Man's Search for Meaning*

Looking at people with ADD as the descendants of Hunters, with a neurochemistry and thalamic gain set-point which causes them to seek stimulation and sensation, puts a lot of behaviors and problems in context. However, there's a third and final step in this perspective which, in part, answers the question: "What can be done to help these low-gain Hunters?"

Stress Responses

When we are faced with danger, real or perceived, we're driven by our reptilian and mammalian brain, which has two primary instincts: fight or flight.

The stress doesn't need to be something as obvious as the danger of a mugger. It can be the fear of being alone or rejected, the fear of not being loved, the fear of failure, the fear of criticism, or anything else that people interpret as a threat or attack.

People with ADD often have a hypervigilant and hyper-responsive stress-sensing mechanism. This may be a vestigial Hunter survival mechanism: if you weren't constantly vigilant in the jungle or forest, you'd get eaten. (This also may partly explain why one of the Adult ADD diagnostic criteria suggested by psychiatrists John Ratey and Edward Hallowell was "A feeling of impending doom." This feeling of doom would spur the hunter to constantly be looking over his shoulder.)

Distractibility- The Effect of Hypervigilance

Whatever the cause or reason, though, the effect of this hypervigilance is what we often call distractibility. The person with ADD is constantly scanning his or her environment for danger. (Distractibility is the first of the three primary characteristics of ADD, the second is impulsivity and the third is sensation/risk-seeking behaviors.)

Impulsivity- A Response to Threat

When the person with ADD senses a real or perceived threat, they tend to have a hair-trigger response to that threat. This often takes the form of interrupting, acting without thinking the consequences through first, or saying or doing whatever comes to mind. While it probably always begins as a response to stress/threat, it may also become a learned behavior which generalizes to other aspects of life. A person can end up responding very quickly to just about any sort of stimuli, including internal ones such as thoughts, impulses, and desires.

Forms of "Flight"

When confronted with a threat or stress, it's usually inappropriate to "fight" in modern society. Punching out the manager who might fire us, throwing something at the person who jumped in front of us in line, or shooting out the windshield of the fellow who cut us off in traffic are generally regarded as less-than-useful behaviors. Most of us have learned to control our response to stress, at least to sublimate the "fight" component of the response.

This leaves us with "flight" as a response. Instead of confronting threats, problems, or individuals whom we perceive as a threat, we usually figure out a way to escape from the source of the stress. Common patterns here include changing relationships frequently, hopping from job to job or even from town to town. Or the pattern may be more subtle than that, because the flight response has two submodalities: run or hide.

When running isn't possible, as is usually the case in "civilized" society, then we often choose to "hide." While for some people this takes an exaggerated form, in such conditions as agoraphobia, where a person is afraid to even leave the house, the hiding behavior more often shows up in people who have learned how to avoid conflict to the point of paralysis, or who seem emotionally unresponsive. This is sometimes seen as a form of coldness or withdrawal, but, paradoxically, in persons with ADD it may often show up as an exaggerated sociability or apparent extroversion. (The reason for this will become clear in a moment.)

Since it's usually difficult to "run away" in modern society, a submode of flight that's commonly used is what I call the "opossum response": overwhelm the brain with stimulation and cause it to be distracted or freed from the source of the stress. When an opossum rolls over and pretends to be dead, it actually slips into a comatose state brought about by the conscious brain being overwhelmed by a flood of sensation from the limbic brain.

Our culture is replete with stories of people who "throw themselves into" things, using work, sex, drugs, alcohol or gambling in order to "get away from" some perceived stress or loss. When taken to an extreme, this throwing oneself into something shows up as addictive, compulsive, or obsessive behaviors, all of which seem to be over-represented among the ADD population.

So we now have a person who is experiencing stress, is incapable of fighting, and can't run away either. In order to cope they choose to hide, to bury themselves within something that's sufficiently strong, high-stimulation, and/or overwhelming providing enough of a distraction to become oblivious to the stress. This is just like the opossum, so deeply gone when "hiding" that he won't respond to being poked, rolled over, or even picked up and dropped.

In order to call up the hiding "opossum response," a person finds either outside or within themselves an overwhelming distraction or point to focus on. It must be something so powerful, so stimulating, and occasionally so rewarding that it exceeds the strength and power of the threat/stress.

Some people with ADD have trained their brains to become very efficient at collecting and seeking out high-energy, high-stimulation, powerfully-overwhelming stimuli. This provides them with a useful catalog of distracting behaviors to fall back into when the opossum response is necessary to flee from stress.

Collection and maintenance of these "distraction tools" show up as risk-taking and sensation-seeking behaviors. Throughout their lives, these individuals have searched for and discovered ways to flood their brains with neurochemicals. We call this "feeling good," or "getting high," and people with ADD are particularly well-tuned to this. These can include sex and masturbation; use of substances such as alcohol, tobacco, coffee, and other harder drugs; gambling; eating; extreme exercise (running, competitive sports); shopping; compulsive talking; compulsive promiscuity; extreme religious behaviors such as joining cults or becoming fanatic evangelists; criminal behaviors; workaholism; and other behaviors described as compulsive or addictive.

So, when stress or threat come along, and fight or flight aren't available, the brain just naturally tumbles into the flight submodality of the opossum response. To do this, it will automatically seek out or roll into one of the modes it has historically used to overwhelm it with stimulation.

In other words, if a person has found that drugs, or sex, or running, or alcohol, or even work have given him or her a high or a strong charge, the brain will remember this and seek out that behavior again in order to bring up a flood of neurochemicals that blocks out the stress. This is why ADD people report that engaging in compulsive or risk-taking behavior "reduces stress" or "relaxes" them, even though these behaviors would be described by a non-ADD person as stressful, frightening, or overwhelming.

When Hiding becomes Addiction or Compulsion

If the stimulus is something that leaves a neurochemical crash afterwards, such as sex, alcohol, gambling, or drugs, among others, the resulting crash will itself then become a new source of stress. This new stress will cause the brain to again look for an overwhelming neurochemical wash, again triggering the behavior. The hangover, the departure of the sexual partner, or the results of the gambling loss, become the trigger, even when the original source of stress is long gone, resolved, or far less threatening than the addiction or behavior itself.

Once trapped into one of these addictive cycles, it's extremely difficult for anybody, and particularly for the hypervigilant/hyper-responsive ADD person to break out of the cycle.

Breaking the Addictive Cycle

Two methods are traditionally used to break this cycle of stress leading to addictive behavior.

The first way is to interrupt the neurotransmitter cycles. This is most often done with drugs such as the SSRIs (Selective Serotonin Re-uptake Inhibitors) such as Prozac, which have been demonstrated to be useful in reducing compulsive, obsessive, and addictive behaviors.

While these drugs have an often miraculous short-term effect on breaking addictive or compulsive behavior patterns, the problem here is that the person is now dependent upon an external chemical. Unless the drug therapy is combined with good psychotherapy, a person hasn't learned new ways to cope with stress or the addiction and so when the chemical is withdrawn the old pattern often emerges with a vengeance.

A second way to break the pattern is to create new responses to stress: give the brain new addictions, essentially, but choose those that hopefully are less destructive than the original ones.

Reports in the psychiatric literature show that this is a strategy the brain will adopt naturally. People in recovery from one addiction often quickly cycle into another one. The most common reports are of people going from substance abuse to sexual compulsion, or from substance abuse to alcohol abuse, although there are legions of examples with virtually every form of compulsive behavior.

These people will universally describe their compulsive substance, alcohol, or sexual acting-out as a response to stress, saying that it makes them feel "relieved," or "calmer," or using other similar terms. The results are unfortunately short-lived however, and a new addiction cycle is merely starting up.

The strategy of replacing one addiction with another (sexual with running, for example) may be useful in preventing people from engaging in self-destructive behavior, but the "new" addiction can often prove destructive itself. Witness the explosion in sports-related injuries from people who say they're "hooked" by the "runner's high," or the number of people in AA who will die from smoking-related illnesses.

There is a third way to break the addictive cycle, and that is by building inner strength.

SOLUTIONS

The Third Way: Building Inner Strength

A third strategy, one that's central to Gestalt therapy but often overlooked in mainstream addiction literature, is to address head-on the hypervigilance and hyperresponsiveness to stress: make a person so strong internally that they no longer need resort to the opossum response.

The basic premise which this strategy is founded on is the realization that much of our response to stress comes from not being in touch with our own inner strengths. We perceive things as stressful because we think of ourselves as weak. After all, who would consider a child on a tricycle to be a threat, unless he thought of himself as an even smaller child? Who would be afraid of losing their job if they were absolutely confident and certain that they could get a better one in a matter of days? Who would be intimidated by somebody physically threatening them if they were a black-belt in karate?

When we operate out of a place of strength, then most things we'd normally find stressful become transformed into non-stressful events. We simply make appropriate choices, deal with them, and go on with life.

Consider the extreme example above of the karate black-belt. Gary Grooms is a Shao Lin martial arts master in Atlanta. He can literally kill a man with his hand, and do it in a matter of seconds. When I asked him how this sort of training transforms people's experience of physical threats (do they get in more fights, for example?), Gary told me something that at first seemed counter-intuitive.

"My students report that they're far less likely to get into a fight once they've mastered our techniques," he told me. "When you know in advance that you're going to win, that you could even seriously damage or kill the other person, then the urge to fight seems to go away. You don't see the other person as a threat anymore, but more like an annoyance or a nuisance, and it's easier to ignore them and carry on with your life."

So a good way to address the hypervigilance and hyper-responsiveness of ADD is to develop a strong inner core, an emotional strength that allows us to brush off the small stresses of life, the way Gary would ignore a rude person at a sporting event. As my mentor Gottfried Müller said, "When you walk through the world as a spiritual warrior, you quickly learn what is important and what you can ignore."

Accessing Our Inner Strengths

The mind organizes itself into separate and discrete areas to deal with life's circumstances. These areas are created, organized, and segregated from the conscious mind during childhood for the largest part, and represent much of what is often referred to as "the unconscious." They work to keep us alive and protected, but because so many of them are created during childhood when cognitive abilities aren't well-developed (regardless of age), they are developed at the level of instinct. These areas of the unconscious that control much of our conscious behavior often appear to act in an irrational fashion.

Thus, someone who is hypercritical of others may have developed this as a way of trying to train *himself* to be more competent. While this may occasionally be useful, more often than not hypercriticalness has destructive consequences. Because it's operating at a level below consciousness, it's nearly impossible to stop it with conscious interventions. Signs on the wall that say "Don't criticize others," or positive-thinking courses, or sessions with a therapist about how your mother was hypercritical herself don't usually produce long-term change.

So, the Third Way is to rewire the brain's response to stress in the first place. This involves two steps:

1. Reach through each of the various stress-response behaviors one at a time and find the inner strength for each that will

enable a person to no longer see those "stress-producing" circumstances in life as being stressful. This acts the same way as the SSRI drugs, in that it breaks the cycle of stress-response-behavior-stress.

2. Give the unconscious mind permission and the ability to come up with new behaviors to use in response to formerly (or currently) stressful situations. When these new behaviors are grounded or rooted in this newly established inner strength, the intermediate behaviors that lead to the addiction/compulsion cycle are then no longer necessary and no longer are summoned by the mind.

Solutions

There is a specific set of steps that a therapist or friend can walk a person through to facilitate this process. I was first exposed to it in 1986 when I was living in Germany and working for the international relief organization, Salem. Herr Müller, Salem's founder (he is now 82), sat me down a week before Christmas in his office and asked what was bothering me. I'd just come back from spending most of November in Beijing studying acupuncture at the international teaching hospital there, and then working with Father Ben Carrion to try to raise money for his program in Manila to help the children living there in the garbage dumps. That had been exciting stuff which I'd enjoyed, but now I was back in Germany where it was gray and cold. I felt, culturally, like an alien and of course I literally was.

Herr Müller just kept asking me why I felt this way, and in response to every answer he would again ask, "Why do you feel that way?" Finally, we hit a bottom-line question where I said that I wanted to feel the presence of God all the time. The next time he probed, suddenly I felt that presence. Herr Müller was playing Handel's *Messiah* in the background as we had the discussion, and to this day I always associate that music with the very real power of the love and presence of God that I felt in his office that day. Since that time, I've brought that feeling and presence into many situations in my life; it's been a constant and powerful and enduring source of strength for me.

You can imagine my surprise when George Lynn, a

psychotherapist in Washington state, suggested I pick up a book called *Core Transformation* by ConnieRae and Tamara Andreas. The book outlines a specific technique, rooted in Neuro Linguistic Programming (NLP) and Gestalt therapy, whereby a person is walked through a certain process. They start with a behavior or feeling they'd like to have better control over or be free from, and then use that behavior the way a deep-sea diver uses an air-hose. This carries a person all the way down through layers of consciousness, behavior, and response to what the Andreas' refer to as a "core state."

This core is the place where a feeling of oneness with God, or infinite bliss, or all-encompassing love lives. The person is then taught to bring that state up through the layers of behavior into their normal waking daily life. While the technique transforms people's specific behaviors (and originally in NLP was probably developed largely just for that purpose), in the Andreas' system that's almost a by-product. The real goal is to dive into the core state, and then bring the power and strength from that back into normal life. It's like becoming a spiritual and emotional black-belt!

While the Andreas' don't specifically address ADD at all in their book, they do talk at length about issues of emotional fragility and building emotional strength. These are often weakness carried around by people with ADD, perhaps as a result of a lifetime of paradox, confusion, and self-doubt. ("I know I'm smart, but then why can't I do well in school?)

This posed for me the question: Could the technique Herr Müller had developed out of his experience as a prisoner-of-war and used on me, and the Andreas sisters had developed out of their training in NLP and Gestalt therapy, be useful in helping people with ADD? Could this help to recover their balance, poise, and internal strength?

In theory, at least, if this system reduces hypervigilance and hyperresponsiveness, then the ADD behaviors of distractibility and impulsivity could be reduced or eliminated. Since the person would now be operating from a sense of strength and core competency rather than hypervigilance and fear, the need for these behaviors would now be gone. Could the result be that their ADD is fully or partly "cured?" Or at the least, could many of the side effects of ADD—the pain and self-loathing and confusion—be resolved?

To test the hypothesis, I got together with a psychotherapist in Atlanta, and we lined up people to do the technique. The results aren't in yet, but the preliminary results are very encouraging. On the other side of the country, George Lynn, the psychotherapist in Washington state, told me that he's been using his version of the Core Transformation technique for some time with ADD patients, and found that it had a significant and positive effect on them.

As you read on into this book, you'll find profiles of many factors which may work individually or together to create the emotional fragility in ADD people which this technique seeks to repair. These are the people who were wounded by being Hunters in a Farmer's world, and through the process of this and other therapies and strategies (many outlined in my previous book, *ADD Success Stories*), I believe it is possible for people with ADD to live successful, fulfilled and empowered lives.

CHAPTER FOUR

Social Adaptations

Few societies have changed the face of the planet and human society as rapidly or radically as has the American culture. Since the founding of this country by the malcontents and misfits of British, and later other national societies, we've innovated and invented.

We invented a new form of government. New technologies. New ways of doing business. And even new social and cultural norms, from the Confederacy to the Flappers of the 1920s to the Hippies to the emerging millennial society. We've created unique forms of music such as Jazz, Blues, Rock & Roll, and Rap, and we've sent men to the moon.

We also have the highest incidence of diagnosed ADD of any society on Earth.

This chapter examines five different aspects of how ADD has shaped our culture, how and why our culture has defined ADD, and what these mean for people with ADD.

ADD Prevents Human Society from Ossifying

"I was born with genes that drive me to get on with doing what has to be done."
— Richard Leakey, *60 Minutes* interview

Another aspect of the way ADD plays out in a cultural context could be set in the framework of the need to reduce uncertainty in life, referenced by various psychological theorists from Adler to Jung.

For those ADDers with a highly-variable sense of time, reducing uncertainty in the environment takes the form of acting *now*, responding immediately to each change in the environment. For those without ADD, however, who experience a linear sense of persisting time, reducing uncertainty takes the form of trying to stabilize things. Those people will, as surely as the tide, eventually try to get rid of people who like to change things.

Thus, because Hunter-like people are the agents of change, once the change they created is adopted by the "stables" (Farmers), this latter group will—as any examination of history shows—isolate them, kill them off, or exile them. Britain did this with those individuals they sent to America and Australia, and we do this socially, ghettoizing ADD children in public schools.

This gives us another insight into a possibly adaptive role for ADD in our modern society.

Certainly, most of modern culture is set up to reward Farmer-like behavior. Our schools are based on an agricultural model, still letting out for the summer, as in times past children were needed to bring in the crops. Stability is cherished and job-hopping and other forms of social instability are viewed as alarm flags to prospective employers or spouses.

The industrial revolution, much like the agricultural revolution, further extended the culture-shift that caused ADD to suddenly fall "outside the template," by introducing mechanization using repetitive (farming) techniques. This helps explain why the "factory" model of modern public schools so often is anathema to ADD children, and why experience-based school environments are so useful for ADD kids.

At first glance, it would seem that being a Farmer in today's society would be very desirable. The checkbook gets balanced, the grass is mowed regularly, and every day the bolt gets put on the screw at the factory, day in and day out.

But it's often the Hunters who are the instruments of social change and leadership. *Societies without Hunters among them require cataclysmic events to stimulate change.*

Japanese society, for example, which had been agricultural for thousands of years, was essentially stagnant until Admiral Perry parked his Black Ships off the coast and threatened war if the Japanese wouldn't let him trade with them.

That signaled the end of a major era in Japanese society. The virtual destruction of Japan during World War II brought about the second great change in their society. It's interesting to note that in the Japanese language there's no word that cleanly translates into "leadership." The notion of standing apart from the crowd, going your own way, and challenging existing institutions is totally alien to Japanese culture. And so we see that virtually all the major changes in that very Farmer-like society were brought about by the invading barbarians (the translation of the Japanese word *gaijin*, which also means foreigner), and happened from without, rather than from within.

On the other hand, the leader in innovation in the world is the United States. We invented the transistor, although the careful and methodical Japanese refined it. The same applies to radio, television, VCRs, plastics, and on and on. We even invented a form of government now duplicated all around the world.

And who were we here in America during our early years, so

innovative as to create an entirely new form of government and numerous inventions? We were the Hunters: misfits of British society daring and brave and crazy enough to undertake the crossing from Europe to America to conquer a new land.

Society needs its Hunters, no matter how much it tries to suppress them in its institutions and schools. ADD Hunters like Edison and Franklin were responsible for massive social, cultural, and technological change, and even today we find a disproportionate number of high-stimulation-seeking persons among the creative ranks, in every discipline from the arts to politics to the sciences.

For example, Wilson Harrell, former publisher of *Inc.* magazine, former CEO of the Formula 409 Corporation, and author of the book *For Entrepreneurs Only* is one of America's most famous entrepreneurs. He teaches companies a new management technique called Total Quality Entrepreneurship, and is a frequent speaker around the world on entrepreneurial issues. After reading the first draft of my book, *Focus Your Energy*, he wrote:

"For generations, we entrepreneurs have been asking ourselves: 'Was I born this way, or was it the circumstances of my childhood that led me to the entrepreneurial life? Was it destiny or accident?'...

"[Now we know that] entrepreneurs are entrepreneurs because, down through the eons of time, we have inherited the Hunter genes of our ancestors....

"Until I read Thom's books, I believed that entrepreneurship was inspired by an insatiable desire for freedom. It's so wonderful to know that it's more, much more. That we are born. That we are genetically bound together. That we can and will pass these incredible genes on to our children and their children's children. That, in spite of politicians and Farmer bureaucracies, the entrepreneurial spirit will live on."

Wilson Harrell views ADD as a net positive, in that it sparks the entrepreneurialism which has made our nation great.

So yet another possible reason for why we have ADD is that it keeps society changing. Without their Hunters, our modern Farmer's societies would become stagnant and technologically primitive.

Solutions

Wilson Harrell has made significant accomplishments in his efforts to help entrepreneurs understand their own ADD-like nature, and to work with the strengths associated with it while avoiding or overcoming the weaknesses. His book *For Entrepreneurs Only* is a great example of this.

Until we have a cultural paradigm shift, however, we'll continue to often label these types of people as disordered when they're really often only different. These differences can keep our society alive, vital, and at the front of progress throughout the world.

Morphic Resonance: The "Hundredth Monkey Phenomenon"

The man who sat on the ground in his tipi meditating on life and its meaning, accepting the kinship of all creatures and acknowledging unity with the universe of things was infusing into his being the true essence of civilization. And when native man left off this form of development, his humanization was retarded in growth.

—Chief Luther Standing Bear

Sir Arthur Eddington, who proved Einstein's theory of relativity by leading the expedition in 1919 to photograph a solar eclipse, was boggled when he saw that gravity did, indeed, bend light. When he realized the implications of Einstein's theory, he wrote: "the stuff of the world is mind stuff," and that "the mind stuff is not spread out in space and time; these are part of the cyclic scheme ultimately derived out of it."

Rupert Sheldrake's concept of morphic resonance proposes that behavior is inherited as an organizing field rather than as a specific genetic encoding. This field is both derived from parents, from self (that is, it accumulates through life), and from others.

This may sound absurd at first, and even Pavlov, when confronted with it, assumed it was a sort of genetic transmission of learned behavior. He trained a group of rats to run to a particular feeding place whenever he rang a bell. The first generation of rats he trained took an average of 300 tries before they learned always to run to the feeding place when Pavlov rang the bell. Their offspring, however, learned how to find the food when the bell was rung after only 100 tries. The children of this second generation got it after thirty tries, and their children learned how to find the food after only ten tries. None were given an opportunity to learn this behavior from their parents, and the results of this study boggled the mind of Pavlov. He died, however, before he was able to follow it up.

But it was followed up, with startling results. From 1920 to 1950, one of the longest studies in the history of behavioral science was conducted at Harvard (and, later, other institutions) by Dr. William McDougal. He put together a test for rats: they were dropped into a darkened tank of cold water from which there were two exit ramps. One ramp was lighted, but gave the rats an electric shock when they tried to use it. The other exit was dark and hard to find, but provided safe escape from the cold water.

Using standard white laboratory rats, McDougal found that the first generation of rats he tested took over 165 tries to master this test. By the time he got to the thirtieth generation, however, the rats easily mastered the test in fewer than 20 tries. When he first published the results of this test, it of course raised skepticism. The idea that behavior might be inherited was odd, to say the least, and more disturbing, might have enlightening or chilling implications if applied to humans.

So biologist F.A.E. Crew tried to replicate McDougal's Harvard experiment in faraway Edinburgh, Scotland. Using the same standard laboratory rats, but ones that had no relation to McDougal's (still in Boston), he found that on the first try his rats could learn the water test with only 25 tries.

The results of this stimulated biologist W.E. Agar in Melbourne, Australia, to try the test out with his rats. He found that the first generation also learned the test in about 25 tries, and as he continued training rats through subsequent generations, he was able to get this down considerably by the fiftieth generation, over twenty years.

What Agar did that was different from Crew or McDougal, however, was that he kept another group of rats breeding in a separate room, unrelated to the test rats, for the same fifty generations without ever giving them any tests or training. When he finally tested his control group, he discovered, to his and everybody else's shock and amazement, that they too learned the maze with a speed identical to offspring of the tested and trained group.

One of the most famous examples of this "remote shared learning" occurred in Britain where for nearly 100 years milkmen have left bottles of milk at homeowner's doors during the dark hours of early morning. In 1921, the first incidence of a small bird opening the top of one of these milk bottles was recorded. It happened in the small town of Southampton, and the bird was the blue tit. By 1947, eleven species of birds had begun this activity, and it had spread to 89 different cities.

Then the jump occurred. A certain critical mass appears to have been achieved in Britain, because suddenly blue tits in Sweden, Denmark, and Holland began to attack milk bottles. It was impossible that this could have been a learned behavior or something that these birds observed.

To further compound the mystery, milk bottles disappeared in Holland during the years of World War II, and were only reintroduced in 1947. None of the blue tits alive then could have ever seen a milk bottle: the last ones placed on doorsteps were during the era of their grandparents or great-grandparents. Yet as soon as the bottles reappeared, the tits began to attack them.

Another well-known story of this phenomenon occurred off the coast of Japan in 1952, on the island of Koshima. Scientists studying the behavior of a local band of monkeys (Macaca fuscata) began feeding them by dropping sweet potatoes on the sand of the beach. The sand made the potatoes difficult to eat, and one young female, Imo, learned to wash the potatoes in the ocean before eating them. She taught this behavior to her friends and relatives, and pretty soon many of the members of this band of monkeys were imitating Imo's food-washing behavior. The scientists observed this with interest, watching how the behavior slowly spread through the tribe, until one day something startling happened: *every* monkey in the tribe began washing their food.

Amazed by this, the scientists reported their observation. At the same time another group of scientists at Takasakiyama on the distant mainland noticed an odd and eerie phenomenon: suddenly all the Macaca fuscata monkeys they were observing began to wash their food in the ocean!

Dr. Rupert Sheldrake calls this phenomena "morphic resonance," and points out several human examples in his book, *The Presence of the Past*. Before 1953, in all of recorded human history, no person had ever run a mile in less than four minutes. This was widely regarded as an unbreakable barrier, having to do with basic laws of physics and human anatomy. Then, in 1954, Roger Bannister ran a mile in under four minutes and shocked the world. The widely-held assumption at the time was that Bannister must have been some sort of a freak, a super-human runner, to have accomplished this feat that everybody knew was patently impossible.

But even more amazing than Bannister having broken the four-minute-mile was the fact that within a year over a dozen people had matched his feat, and within a decade over a thousand had. By 1985, the "barrier" was redefined by Steve Cram, who ran the mile in 3 minutes 46.3 seconds. That this feat was duplicated not just in Bannister's native England but all over the world is testament to the fact that this didn't represent some sudden evolution in the technology of running shoes or human nutrition. It was the newly-shared knowledge that to do this was possible.

Extending this to learning, studies were done with non-Japanese speaking students in England and the United States who were presented with two poems in Japanese. One poem was a classic nursery rhyme known to millions of Japanese and the other a "made-up" rhyme similar in structure and form. The students were able to memorize the "real" poem 62% more easily and faster than the made-up rhyme.

They tested to see if this effect was merely the result of the real rhyme having survived some sort of natural selection process in Japan because it was somehow structurally or intrinsically easier to learn. Yale professor of psychology Dr. Gary Schwartz put together three sets of seemingly nonsense words, each made up of three characters. One set was 24 3-character words in Hebrew which were common in the Old Testament. The second set was 24 3-character Hebrew words which were rare in the Bible. And the third set weren't Hebrew words at all, but scrambled anagrams of the first two sets, comprising 48 nonsense words structurally similar to the two sets of real words.

These 96 words were then randomly projected on a screen, and students were asked to guess at their meaning, and also to rank how confident they felt that they'd guessed right. None of the students had any knowledge of or background in Hebrew.

Dr. Schwartz was impressed to discover a "highly significant statistically" result. The students felt far more confident about their guesses when they were looking at real words and they were more than twice as likely to feel that way when looking at the common real words rather than the uncommon ones.

A similar test using Persian words in Arabic script was performed in England by psychologist Alan Pickering, with similar results.

The concept of people having shared memories or knowledge isn't new, although the scientific validation of it is. Gestalt psychology has long held that there is a psychological field that people are immersed in, and Carl Jung saw this in his concept of the psychological archetype. Prior to the many scientific experiments recently and currently being carried out to test the hypothesis of morphic resonance, this was largely kept in the realm of metaphysics, with proponents such as Edgar Cayce, or as a core concept in the religions of Hinduism and Buddhism.

But now it's widely becoming accepted that what author Ken Keyes called the "Hundredth Monkey Phenomena" is real. If this is the case, when a certain critical mass of people engage in a particular type of behavior that behavior then becomes universalized, spreading to other humans all over the world. Might not this be a possible explanation for the explosion of ADD?

American and Australian societies, pioneering being in their core nature, are vastly more ADD-friendly than stable agricultural societies such as Japan. As the populations of these nations increase, with the numbers of ADD-type individuals growing, one could hypothesize that this would create what Sheldrake calls a Morphogenic Field for ADD behaviors. This field, once it reaches a particular strength, would then have the ability to influence other humans, causing them to behave in a more ADD-like fashion than they might have otherwise done.

So here is another possible explanation for the seeming explosion of ADD, if a bit more esoteric than the usual. Perhaps
we've all just tuned into a new morphic field!

Solutions

This view of ADD implies that ADD may not be a disorder or
disease. It may simply be a normal variation of human behavior
that, during the tens or hundreds of thousands of years of human
history, has been more or less useful. At the heyday of the agricultural and industrial revolutions, with their armies and pesticides
and destruction of natural environments becoming more
anachronistic, it may be that ADD is again useful. And, as there is
more ADD-like behavior, more people tune into the ADD Morphogenic field—leading to even more ADD. Solution? Maybe this
isn't a problem, but a solution for the future of the world in and
of itself.

"Normal" People Are Really "Abnormal"

"Consistency is contrary to nature, contrary to life. The only completely consistent people are dead."

—Aldous Huxley

There's an old cliché to the effect that in the land of the blind, the one-eyed man is king. Similarly, in a land of jewelers, the farsighted man is disabled, whereas in the world of sailing ship lookouts the nearsighted man is disabled. Among basketball players, being under six feet tall is a disability, whereas among football players it's a disability to be tall and skinny.

So what's normal and what's a disability?

We know that if a person uses a particular muscle group heavily, that particular part of the body will strengthen and swell. This is the basis of body-building. We also know that when particular parts of the brain are used a lot, they grow: blood vessels increase in size and number, and the actual size of the brain area and number of interconnections in it increases.

So what if the people without ADD are the abnormals, the mutants, as it were, and those with ADD are the human norm?

This may sound fantastic at first, what with ADD being considered a disability or a disorder, but consider the world in which we live.

Dr. Marc Lappé says in *Evolutionary Medicine: Rethinking the Origins of Disease*, "My premise is simple—most medical problems are problems of evolution." He goes on to show how the world in which earlier humans lived for hundreds of thousands of years is radically different from that in which we've spent the past few hundred years. Many of the "diseases" of modern life—ranging from diabetes to sickle-cell anemia—were once really useful. "Given the radical transformations of environments by humankind, we can expect that many human 'adaptations' are not well-suited to contemporary circumstances. In a more extreme sense, certain previously adaptive traits are now maladaptive..."

Although this demonstrates the basis of my Hunter/Farmer theory, let's flip it upside-down.

Modern society requires a level of self-control probably unknown in primitive societies. Hunter-gatherers of 20,000 years ago didn't have to wait for traffic lights, sit in doctor's waiting rooms, or suffer through boring classrooms listening to subjects of dubious relevance. Their world was more immediate and reaction-driven, and scanning/distractibility and quick decision-making/impulsivity were useful assets.

But modern society requires patience. It requires a level of self-control and discipline largely unseen in primitive societies. We must learn to postpone gratification, to think in terms of times which may extend for years or even generations, and to control even our most subtle nuances of expression in some social, school, or business situations.

This is highly abnormal for any animal, including humans.

We see evidence of the difficulty of such behavior in such statistics as the doubling of the rates of depression in industrialized countries roughly every ten years. Suicide is the third most common cause of death among young adults, and fifteen percent of Americans have been treated for a clinical anxiety disorder.

Freud pointed to this in his book, *Civilization and Its Discontents*, when he noted that although we are told to love our neighbor, our modern society instead drives us to "humiliate him, to cause him pain, to torture and to kill him." Freud concluded that modern civilization had created "Homo homini lupus": man is the wolf to man.

Even the Unabomber both illustrates and asserts evidence of this. In his 35,000 word essay published in the *Washington Post*, he noted that "[I] attribute the social and psychological problems of modern society to the fact that society requires people to live under conditions radically different from those under which the human race evolved..."

Yet when anthropologists set out to determine the rate of depression among the primitive Kaluli people of New Guinea, they were unable to detect any. Similarly, rural Samoan villagers have extraordinarily low levels of cortisol in their blood, a chemical considered an accurate marker for levels of anxiety.

The agricultural revolution is considered by many to be a huge evolutionary leap in human society. The *Cambridge Encyclopedia of Human Evolution* rates it as, "after fire, mankind's greatest harnessing of the world's natural energy. It certainly led to changes, setting the stage for the more recent industrial revolution."

But some look less kindly on the results of the agricultural revolution, and the type of people who emerged during it and then proceeded to wipe out 98% of all the hunter-gatherer humans who then populated the earth.

In the book *The Third Generation*, Jared Diamond suggests the agricultural revolution was in many ways a negative turning point in human history. It brought about, he says, the "gross social and sexual inequality, the disease and despotism, that curse modern human existence." Diamond pointed out that along with these social ills came physical ills as well. Hunter-gatherer era skeletons of American Indians dug up in the Illinois and Ohio River valleys differ so dramatically from the later, smaller, and less healthy agriculture era skeletons in the same region that Diamond called corn, often thought to be an agricultural wonder, "a public health disaster."

But once people lived on the same piece of land for generations, elite hierarchies developed within groups and wars broke out for control of the food-producing land. While agriculture led to Athenian notions of democracy and the Renaissance, it also gave us standing armies of professional killers, Diamond points out.

During the Hunter-gatherer era, anthropological evidence suggests men and women had more equal roles in terms of the power and politics of the tribe. In *Food In History*, Reay Tannahill points out that the cultivation of crops "increased women's burdens while it lightened man's." Tannahill added that while women bore the brunt of the agricultural work, men were "released from the physical and mental strains of the hunt to the peaceable tending of his flocks, which gave him both time and opportunity for constructive thinking, formulating plans, setting up and attending village councils, and criticizing women's lack of inventiveness' in the matter of crop-raising."

Solutions

We in Western society live in a disordered world, from the viewpoint of the evolution of our species. We must learn a whole new set of behaviors, and incorporate them thoroughly to become part of our nature.

Since science tells us that these behaviors are mostly controlled by the right frontal lobes of the brain, it would make sense that a person who had successfully adapted to modern society—mutated from the human norm—would have an abnormally large right frontal lobe. And that, of course, is exactly what the National Institutes of Mental Health found when they compared the brains of "normal" and "ADD" children: the normals had slightly enlarged right-front lobes.

So perhaps we have ADD because those with ADD haven't yet made the transition necessary for life in post-agricultural revolution, post-industrial revolution society. Either for lack of early exercise of those parts of their brains, or because of a genetic predisposition not to be strong in that area, they haven't mutated into the new "Homo modernus."

Alternatively, it may be that those without ADD are the ones who are doomed as we move into a brand-new era of radical and rapid change. Although ideally suited to the agricultural revolution, able to extend from one continent to another, murdering and conquering everything and everybody in their path, "Farmers" may in the next century find themselves at a mental disadvantage. The ADD individuals may thrive in the Information Age, or in the chaos that some predict will engulf the earth as the surplus of people and shortage of oil and other natural resources collide in the next few decades.

To the extent that it's possible, then, modern people with

ADD who live in Western society have two options: find a niche in society which is more Hunter-like, or learn to at least behave like Homo modernus. The former has to do with job and lifestyle choices, as I've outlined in considerable detail in previous books (particularly *Focus Your Energy: Hunting For Success In Business With ADD*) The latter includes learning about new work and lifestyle strategies, ways to retrain the brain such as meditation or EEG Neurofeedback, and possibly medications that alter brain chemistry to make it more similar to Homo modernus.

Our Culture is Increasingly Intolerant of "Different" People

"The ae half of the world thinks thither daft."
— Sir Walter Scott, *Redgauntlet*

When we moved to rural New Hampshire in 1978, we were assured that we'd soon be accepted by the locals. "It'll only take twenty or thirty years for them to consider you one of us," the local chief of police told me. "Until then, though, you're an outsider. And that's about as close to 'the enemy' as one can be."

I now live in Atlanta, and the people with a southern accent look down on the "carpetbaggers" from the north, while the transplants from other parts of the country tend to react to a southern twang as a sign of stupidity or lack of culture. There's even a school here in Atlanta which does nothing but teach southerners how to speak without their accent.

But this just scratches the surface.

Not only are people different in the ways they speak and the general lifestyles they find comfortable, they're also different in the way they think, the way their minds are organized. One of the most articulate spokespeople for those with brains that are "unconventionally organized" is Judith Kolberg, an Atlanta professional organizer. She teaches seminars, does consulting, and even publishes tapes and booklets on her systems.

In one of her tapes, she points out that most people think of filing as linear, sequential, and hierarchical. Things are put in folders according to nouns—their categories—and are then sub-filed according to their sub-categories.

This works fine for people who are linear thinkers, points out Kolberg, but it does nothing at all for people whose minds don't operate in this linear, hierarchical fashion. So she's developed a radical new system for filing: use verbs! In one of her systems, file folders might be labeled "Call," or "Write Back," or "Copy," or "Pay."

She also notes that some people respond best to organizational systems based on feelings, instead of categories or actions. For those people, files may be labeled, "Worry About This," "Deal with this later," or "Stay out of jail" (where one client filed his IRS and child-support stuff).

What Kolberg has pinpointed is that not everyone's brains work alike. "These types of alternative filing systems are particularly useful for my clients who've been diagnosed with ADD," says, further demonstrating the differences between how people think.

The problem is that society, office, jobs, and schools are all geared toward linear, hierarchical systems—devised years ago by logical, white, middle-class, left-brain men. But when people with differently-organized brains try to use these systems, they inevitably have problems.

Bosses, teachers, and even spouses are often brutally intolerant of non-normal thinking, behaving, and learning styles. When people with different styles are forced to do things in the conventional way, they fail—and that failure is then pointed to with an "ah, ha!" as proof that the person has some sort of a disorder.

The simple fact, though, is that everybody is different in one way or another, both on the outside and the inside. Yet we often have cruel labels for these differences. Historically in our male-dominated society, a woman who has a lower sex drive than her husband is called "frigid"; a person who prefers relationships with others of his or her own gender is "homosexual," and denigrating epithets like fag or queer are thrown like stones; minorities are niggers, chinks, wops, hymies, spics, and the like; and even kids with ADD are often singled out in school by their peers and referred to derisively as "ADDers," or "hypers." The "new right" has managed to make the old badge of pride, Liberal, into a curse word, while those on the left often refer to conservatives as neocons or Nazis. Political demagogues love to use the word "them" in speeches to whip up the crowd, implying that some people out there are insidiously different from "us."

Given all this, it's small wonder that, in the search to find those who are different, children and adults who think or behave in unconventional ways would be labeled "disordered." After all, they're not "normal," are they? Of course, neither were those who disagreed with Hitler or Stalin or Joe McCarthy.

There's probably a good and healthy reason for this. A few thousand years ago, virtually all humans lived tribally, and people within a tribe were genetically similar. Because they shared a strong common ancestry, they looked and even acted in similar fashion. When another tribe came along, it usually wasn't to make friends but to steal resources, food, land, women, money, etc.. So people built castles, formed governments and armies, and developed an instinctive wariness of anybody who wasn't similar to themselves.

This need for similarity is rooted deep in our psyche and is borne out by studies that show people who are happily married long-term are more likely to have identical spacing between their eyes and identical lengths of their middle fingers. As peculiar as this may seem, it's a very real statistic, showing that people become most intimate with others who have some (but not too much) genetic similarity.

So it may be that some of the explosion of ADD diagnoses we're seeing is the simple result of the normal and human instinct to look for, be wary of, or even suppress, enslave, and disempower "them."

Solutions

Judith Kolberg offers a number of brilliant and useful solutions to this situation with her "radical" organizing systems.

Thomas Edison found he was most creative when waking up from a short nap. Instead of sleeping through the night in a bed he often cat-napped on a couch with a few marbles in his hand, hanging off the edge of the sofa. When he finally dozed off, the marbles would fall from his hand into a pie-pan, creating a clatter that would awaken him into what he considered his most creative and insightful state.

John Kennedy hated desks and did his best and most creative writing in the White House sprawled on the floor with his feet on a couch and a legal pad on his chest.

One solution to this round-peg/square-hole problem is for people to abandon their efforts to force themselves into society's neat little niches. Feel free to seek your own creative, unconventional, but functional solutions!

Another solution is for all of us, as a society, to become more tolerant of individual differences. Tell the demagogues and diagnosticians who would cast as ill and disordered huge segments of humanity that they should first look at the beams in their own eyes.

The Perception of Time

Time is but the stream I go a-fishing in.

—Thoreau, *Walden*

Philosophers and scientists have examined for millennia both the way we perceive and the way we move through time. Some have characterized it as standing in a river while time flows by us, or floating down the river of time as the world (past) moves by us. Others talk about the past and future as non-existent, that we only live in the present. Time is an illusion of our minds: there is only the perpetual *now.*

Einstein referred to time as a function of, and relative to, motion and space, leading to his theory of time dilation. Some of his followers have characterized it as a deformation in the curvature of space, or vice-versa.

Regardless of what time is, one thing that seems true for the vast majority of ADD adults is that they experience the passage of it in a fashion different from that of "normal" individuals.

I first wrote about this phenomenon back in 1992 in *Attention Deficit Disorder: A Different Perception.* Russell Barkley, in a chapter of an anthology on ADD that Janie Bowman and I edited titled *Think Fast: The ADD Experience,* put forth his belief that our frontal lobes, where the passage of time is perceived, may be involved in what we call ADD. At the time that I wrote of people with ADD perceiving time differently it wasn't part of the diagnostic criteria for ADD and still isn't. Literally hundreds of ADD adults, however, have written or spoken to me since that first book came out to say that they experience exactly what I described.

They agree that this variable perception of the passage of time may in some fundamental way be involved in bringing about what we call ADD.

For most individuals with ADD, there are only two times: now, and some other time. This leads to procrastination. "Is it 'now' yet? It's not? I guess I can wait..." It also leads to tardiness. At least a dozen ADDers I know have the nickname "the late so-and-so" and last-minute binges of work and school assignments are common, with a perpetual rush-rush to catch up.

These people also report that when they're on the hunt, or really interested in something, time seems to move very quickly. When they're bored, however, or waiting for gratification, time grinds to such a crawl that it's emotionally and sometimes even physically painful.

ADD lay expert Dave deBronkart commented on this phenomenon in a discussion on the ADD Forum on CompuServe. He said:

"Maybe NOW is, in human life, not a point in time but a small "bubble" that does have a start and an end, so there's some depth to "now." I suspect our presence in time isn't a "flat" slice but more like a streamlined teardrop shape.

"A key factor could be the width of different people's 'ovals' or their path through the perception of time. For instance, depth perception' of time (the ability to sense how far away something is) might come from the differences perceived between the front of the oval and the back of it. A person whose oval is flat might not have much of that sense."

He continues, "For a real kick, what if you take the oval and rotate it 90 degrees? Maybe in the other direction it's flat. What you'd then get would be someone who doesn't perceive much from moment to moment, but who perceives an extraordinary amount 'all at once.'

"And that, of course, is what's often said about successful ADDers and Hunter/entrepreneurs: an incomprehensible ability to do many things at once, or to integrate ideas from wildly unrelated disciplines. (Edison often referred to his 'kaleidoscopic' brain.)"

The reasons for this difference in the perception of time between "normal" and ADD people are unknown.

Some say these differences in the perception and awareness of time came about as a result of the agricultural revolution and therefore represent a refinement in the brain that allowed humans to become farmers. This would imply that those persons who don't have the "Farmer time sense" are evolutionary throwbacks, prehistoric relics who somehow stumbled through the course of evolution and natural selection into today's world.

On the other hand, some futurists and ADD skeptics like Dr. Thomas Armstrong assert that what we're calling ADD might actually represent an evolutionary improvement or necessary variation in humanity, with which our institutions have simply not yet caught up. Certainly a nation of obedient, compliant, "perfect student" children would be radically different from that in which we live. We'd probably still be a colony of Great Britain, lacking electric lights, the phonograph, motion pictures, and thousands of other things brought into life by "eccentric" inventors who easily fit the psychiatric criteria for ADD.

Futurist John Naisbitt in his ground breaking book *Mega-Trends* proposes that in the near future people won't just change jobs through their adult lifetimes, but will frequently change *careers*, often as many as seven times, something relatively "normal" for ADD adults.

Solutions

If time is not "real" but instead just a perception, a creation of our minds or something which can only be subjectively known, then it makes perfect sense that the Hunter's time-variable mind would be an advantage in the information age. The same mind which could slow time when the prey was spotted during the hunt and speed it up while on the chase could similarly adapt to the Internet, video games, driving in urban America, and the rapid pace of modern business.

As Wilson Harrell, former publisher of *Inc. magazine and president of the Formula 409 company, put it: "ADD is a survival skill in the rough-and-tumble world of entrepreneurial business, just as it is on the battlefield. You have to learn to think fast when necessary, and think slow when that's called for as well. Time must be a pressure like the wind at your back."*

So the best solution here is to make the transition from the Agricultural Age/Industrial Age to the Information Age...and leave all those Farmers and factory workers behind.

CHAPTER FIVE

The Stress and Toxicity of Modern Life

While there may be a "pure" form of ADD in which all the symptoms and signs are clear-cut and easily defined, most practitioners would tell you that it only exists in textbooks. ADD is both a complex and a slippery diagnosis, and there are many things which can masquerade as it, exacerbate it, or even cause it to be overlooked when it's a significant problem.

This chapter looks primarily at some of the environmental factors we face—from toxic substances in our air and water to nutrient-depleted food to the breakdown of society in what some think are the "Last Days"—as contributing factors to both ADD itself and to the increasing numbers of ADD diagnoses.

Much of it is highly speculative, but it's my hope it'll provide you with a rich basket of food for thought.

Our Toxic Environment Neurologically Damages Fetuses

"In health there is freedom. Health is the first of all liberties."
— Henri-Frederic Amiel, 1828-1881

Perhaps another reason why we see so much behavior that looks like, or is misdiagnosed as ADD is because more and more of us are growing up in a neurologically toxic environment.

In most of the world, lead is still added to gasoline. Only in the past few decades has it been removed from the fuel of the industrialized nations. Lead-contaminated paint can be found in many homes, particularly older ones, more likely to be occupied by low-income people. Children in the inner cities consistently test out as having high levels of lead in their bloodstream.

This is significant because there's a direct correlation between lead levels in the bloodstream and the ability to perform well on intelligence tests and in school. While severe lead poisoning can cause profound retardation or other obvious neurological damage, it's been learned in the past twenty years that even small amounts of lead will have a subtle but measurable effect on the ability to develop and function mentally.

Similarly, at the October, 1995 International Conference on Toxicology held in Hot Springs, Arkansas, researchers reported on 17-year follow-up studies of 2000 residents of central Taiwan. They were exposed to high levels of polychlorinated biphenyl's (PCBs), a chemical so widely used for the past six decades for electrical transformers and other applications that it can be found in the blood of nearly every human on earth.

These Taiwanese, from the Yu Cheung area were exposed to levels of PCB that were, on average, about fifty times that of the average world citizen. Their children, born after the chemical spill in the area, were found to have levels around six times higher than normal. These children exhibited "small but significant delays in attaining normal developmental milestones" in childhood, and the boys performed poorly on reasoning tests. They also found, oddly, that these PCB-exposed children were six times as likely as normal Taiwanese children to suffer from recurrent ear infections, an odd anomaly often noted among ADD-diagnosed children in the United States.

The neurological effects of toxins may not be limited to exotic and deadly chemicals in our environment. In R. Ridley and H.F Baker's 1983 paper, "Is there a relationship between social isolation, cognitive inflexibility and behavioral stereotypy? An analysis of the effects of amphetamine in the marmoset," and in K.A. Miczek's (ed), "Ethopharmacology: Primate Models of Neuropsychiatric Disorders" a case is made that stimulant drugs taken during pregnancy may profoundly affect the developing fetus. Other researchers have wondered out loud whether this may even extend to caffeine, although it's difficult and politically unwise to try to get research money for studying the effects of that drug.

Twenty years ago no one warned pregnant mothers that alcohol and nicotine could damage their unborn child: now such warnings are commonplace. Forty years ago DDT was routinely dusted on virtually every food we ate, and sold as a garden powder. Now it's banned worldwide, but still shows up in the fat of Antarctic seals. Lead was put into gasoline and paint for nearly a century before it was learned that just these two environment sources of lead were reducing IQ scores among city-dwelling children by as much as 10 points.

Solutions

We must be careful not to fall into the trap of assuming that our current state of knowledge about the toxicity of our environment is the end-state of all knowledge. Yesterday's health-food fad is often today's practical reality or EPA law.

It may seem a bit eccentric to shop in the organic produce section, or to insist that our children eat their vegetables. When our houses are not full of junk foods and sugary breakfast cereals, however, it may provide our children with that small edge they'll need to grow up with a strong nervous system in an increasingly complex and demanding world.

Nutritional Deficiencies

That we can feed this mind of ours is a wise passiveness.
—William Wordsworth, *Expostulation and Reply*

Serotonin is one of the primary neurotransmitters that facilitates and regulates our ability to think, to pay attention, and to engage in higher mental functions. It also plays a strong role in our emotional state: when levels are out of balance people will fall into depression, mania, and a host of emotional symptoms between the two.

Given the importance of this neurotransmitter in maintaining normal functioning of the brain and emotional systems, we would be remiss if we didn't look at those ecological factors proven to affect serotonin levels or the ability of the brain to use serotonin.

Vitamin E: In a study published in 1992 in *The Journal of Neurochemistry*, researcher Dr. A. Castano found that as little as two weeks on a vitamin-E deficient diet was enough to damage the serotonin-processing neurons in the brains of rats. This was corroborated in a study published in *Brain Research* in 1993.

Vitamin C: The body uses vitamin C in the process of manufacturing serotonin. While the recommended daily allowance (RDA) of vitamin C is 60 milligrams per day, this may be far less than optimal. One 10-year study reported in *Beyond Prozac* by Michael J. Norden, M.D., found that men who consumed 400 milligrams or more daily had 70 percent less mortality than men who consumed 50 milligrams.

Minerals: Lithium is the treatment of choice for people suffering from bipolar disorder (manic-depressive illness). It's also a naturally-occurring mineral found in varying levels in much soil. Scientists knew from their studies with sufferers of bipolar disorder that lithium tablets would increase serotonin levels, but were astounded when they looked at psychiatric and criminal statistics from those parts of the country where the soil lithium levels are so high as to be measurable in drinking water (principally in Texas). They discovered significantly lower levels of suicide, drug abuse, alcoholism, and a host of other psychiatric illnesses. A number of studies have all but proven that this is attributable only to the trace levels of lithium in the local food and water.

Similarly, chromium, zinc, manganese, copper, and iron are all minerals necessary for the manufacture and maintenance of proper brain levels of serotonin.

Vitamin B6: This vitamin is the most directly tied into the serotonin system, as it's required to convert dietary L-tryptophan into serotonin. Studies have found that high levels of it are therapeutic in a number of serotonin-related disorders, including depression and seizures.

The significance of all these nutrients in the context of ADD is that they're all necessary in appropriate amounts for normal brain function. The way most people get them is through the foods they eat, yet much of our food has lost virtually all of its nutrients. We take wheat, for example, strip out the germ (the budding plant at the center which has the highest levels of nutrients and vitamin E), the bran, and then chemically bleach the resulting starchy substance left. This destroys virtually all the nutrients except the starch, producing the nice, white flour that seems to be so loved by so many ADD kids. Similarly, sugar cane juice has all its minerals and vitamins removed (the removed goo of its nutrients is molasses), and is then chemically bleached to remove whatever might have escaped the primary extraction process.

Cooking destroys many nutrients, and others are leached out of foods into cooking water which usually is thrown away.

Solutions

The bottom line is that many experts in nutrition—and not just those from the "health food fringe"—believe that Americans are among the worst-nourished people in the industrial world because of our heavy reliance on processed foods.

Vitamins and minerals have been aggressively stripped from our soil and foods, and then trace amounts of a small spectrum of "essential" nutrients are added back (sometimes by requirement of law, so bad was the damage done to people in the early years of this century by eating processed food). This however, is no solution. People must eat a diet rich in raw or lightly cooked fruits, vegetables, and whole grains if they are to expect their bodies— and their brains—to function properly.

Ritalin is Such a Cool Drug

With pleasure drugged, he almost longed for woe, And e'en
for change of scene would seek the shades below.
— Byron: *Child Harold*, Canto 1, st. 6

This theory of why there's such an explosion of ADD has more to do with the proliferation of the diagnosis among adults than it does among children.

Children often report they don't like the way Ritalin makes them feel, or are resentful about having to take anything at all. Particularly after the first few months when the newness of the experience has worn off, it's just another thing to have to remember. Children also simply appreciate that it helps them do better in school.

But among adults, although these same responses are common, another response occurs with alarming frequency.

Literally hundreds of adults have come up to me at ADD conferences, book signings, ADD support group meetings, or other public events and begun what we used to call back in the '60s a "speed rap." The person talks so fast that they barely can keep up with their own words. They smile widely, have great urgency and intensity, and often bounce up and down while talking. They have an absolute certainty that they're saying the most important words ever uttered in the history of humankind, and that their insights are mind-boggling and world-changing. They believe the person they're talking to is hanging on their every phrase.

Sometimes it's amusing; more often than not it's annoying to the other people who want a book signed or have a question to ask. When I spoke in 1995 to a convention for adults with ADD, I encountered at least two or three speed-rappers an hour throughout the day. One fellow even paused in mid-sentence of a mind-numbing discourse about the state of American politics (he'd stopped me in the hall to share his insights about Bill Clinton's ADD) to throw down his throat a half-dozen yellow 5 mg. tablets of Ritalin.

"How much of that stuff do you take?" I asked.

"Not much," he said. "Only about a hundred-fifty milligrams a day." While this may seem like an eye-popping amount of stimulant to take (normally, adults and children begin at 10 to 30 mg./day), there has been quite a bit of discussion lately on CompuServe's ADD Forum about the value of such high doses of methylphenidate (Ritalin), Dexedrine, or amphetamine. No doubt some folks require such high doses. If nothing else, the spectrum of humanity varies widely in its neurochemistry.

But there's also a problem here: some of these people have gone from unhappy and dysfunctional to bubbling and dysfunctional. While from the inside it may seem like an improvement to them, follow-up discussions with many reveal that they experience black depressions when they "crash" from their high levels of drugs. Therefore, some are also on antidepressants such as Prozac. And most distressing, very, very few are receiving any sort of psychotherapy or learning new life skills to help them become more functional with or without medication.

Several psychiatrists commonly on the ADD speaking circuit have shared with me similar observations. A small but measurable subgroup of adults really enjoy the buzz they get from stimulants and whether they're ADD or not, they're using an ADD diagnosis to maintain access to these substances.

This certainly wouldn't be the first time that a drug drove the diagnosis of mental conditions (rather than the other way around, as one would normally expect). Sigmund Freud found cocaine so psychologically liberating that for several years he prescribed it to nearly all his patients, as well as taking it himself. Until the darker side of the drug revealed itself to him, Freud believed it facilitated the cure of conditions ranging from depression to sexual dysfunction.

When I was a college student we all knew of several area

physicians who'd willingly prescribe diet pills for anybody as much as ten pounds over the norm. We regularly used those diet pills instead as study aids: they were, after all, the same stimulant drugs now used to treat ADD. The availability of stimulant drugs drove an epidemic of overweight diagnoses. And this wasn't just limited to college students in Michigan. Housewives and young women across America had discovered diet pills in the '60s, leading to an entire American subculture of middle-class drug-users chronicled in books and movies such as *Valley of the Dolls*.

It's impolitic to say that people take drugs simply because they enjoy them, but it's a widespread fact of life. Look at the millions of Americans who take nicotine in the form of tobacco, a drug which when taken as directed often leads to death. Alcohol is another recreational drug of our culture. The way that over-the-counter drugs are pushed on TV, it's easy to understand how the average raised-on-television American might think that there's a pill to solve virtually every problem.

With the stimulant drugs used for ADD, there's a substantial grain of truth to the notion that they solve a problem. Benzedrine was first promoted in the 1930's by Dr. Bradley as the "miracle mathematics pill," and thousands of college students took it to improve their test scores. Dexedrine and Benzedrine were routine-ly given by the U.S. military to pilots from the late 1930s until the practice was mentioned on CNN during the Gulf War and then discontinued because of the adverse publicity. These drugs do measurably enhance performance, at least over the short term.

So here is another possible reason why so many people are visiting the doctor to inquire about having ADD. Stimulant drugs produce an enjoyable sensation and make some people more proficient—at least over the short term—at their work or studies.

Solutions

A recent study on drinkers of coffee found that nurses who consumed more than two cups of coffee daily were less likely to commit suicide than those who consumed less than two cups. Although this study was flawed in several significant ways (it didn't look at personality factors which may be common to non-coffee-drinkers and suicidal people, for example, or between coffee-drinkers and non-suicidal people), it may indicate that there's some benefit in taking stimulant drugs on a regular basis.

So the solution to this situation may be twofold:

First, consider that the drug may be driving the diagnosis, and look for other ways people can find satisfaction in life without using Ritalin or other stimulants. These would include the standard psychotherapeutic strategies of examining the life situation, relationships, work, etc., and looking for better alternatives or ways to change. Many of these are outlined in my previous book, *ADD Success Stories.*

And second, perhaps we should reconsider the role that Ritalin and other stimulants play in our society, and the level of restriction attendant to them. While the first strategy implies using less of these drugs, it may also be indicated that there should be more use of them, particularly the naturally-occurring compounds such as caffeine and Gingko.

Life in America (and the Rest of the Industrialized World) is Getting Crazy

Lo! thy dread empire, Chaos! is restor'd;
Light dies before thy uncreating word:
Thy hand, great Anarch! lets curtain fall;
And Universal Darkness buries All.

—Pope, *Dunciad*

Not since the Great Depression have we had so many children dropping out of or failing in school or so many people homeless. Now we also have the highest percentage and the highest raw numbers of incarcerated citizens in the world. And finally, never have so many people exhibited or been diagnosed with mental disorders.

ADD (diagnosed or undiagnosed) may be one of the more common causes of school failure. There also may be a causal correlation between the high percentage of people in prison who could be or are diagnosed with ADD and the crimes of impulse or substance abuse which landed them in jail. Might all this then have to do with the state of modern life?

To those familiar with the topic, it may seem silly to position some ADD as merely a product of our stressful times. After all, we have specific criteria for ADD, and have even tentatively shown differences in brain function between ADD and non-ADD individuals.

Yet long-term stress can produce measurable and definable changes in the body and brain, and those changes may become permanent over time. First documented in rat studies in the early decades of this century, more recent research into stress has given us startling insights into how stress affects the body and mental functioning.

Endocrinologist Dr. Hans Selye of the Institute on Experimental Medicine and Surgery in Montreal was the first person to describe and define the condition known as "human stress." He points out that the stress syndrome is not a mental or emotional condition, but an actual physiological response of the body. It's not the same thing as depression, frustration, anxiety, or worry, although in the popular press these are often miscast as stress.

Instead, stress produces specific and measurable changes in the autonomic and sympathetic nervous system, including the release of adrenaline and noradrenaline, glucose from the liver, dilation of the bronchi and pupils, changes in clotting processes, increases in the number of leukocytes, and changes in cholesterol levels. When stress is severe and sustained, there are also changes in cortisone levels which can lead to physical and mental function changes, including modification of the attention span. In fact, a medical textbook used in most medical schools, *Harrison's Principles of Internal Medicine*, speculates that as many as 50% to 80% of all physical diseases seen in doctor's offices are either psychosomatic or stress-related in their origin.

If stress is capable of producing lasting and destructive physical and mental changes, where is the stress coming from that would be so severe and pervasive? Might it account for some percentage of the explosion in what is diagnosed as ADD?

Collapse of the Middle Class

A major national survey conducted in 1995 found that anxiety was the most pervasive emotion people described in America, according to the Associated Press. The article by Washington reporter Mike Feinsilber pointed out that three out of four Americans surveyed said they were dissatisfied with the direction of life in America, a record.

Feinsilber quoted Jerome Segal, a philosopher at the University of Maryland's Institute for Philosophy and Public Policy, noting that what were once considered basic necessities of life in

America—decent housing, transportation, schooling, and health care—are increasingly out of the reach of the middle class.

For example, Segal pointed out that a smaller percentage of people today have decent housing than did Americans 50 years ago. This is largely because many American cities have deteriorated since 1980 to the point where they're virtual war zones, yet still are primary locations for business and commerce. So residents must either flee to the suburbs and then endure long, stressful daily commutes to work, or else pay a premium for in-town housing that often carries with it an added and stressful risk of crime.

Similarly, this move to the suburbs means that the family car has become a necessity to commute to work, and because so many families now have two people working, two cars are required. The financial burden and the added commute time increases family stress as one or both parents are gone from home for long periods.

Schools have turned into war zones in the inner cities, and many suburbs aren't faring much better. A look at any week's local evening news will find stories even in mid-sized cities, of violent crime in the schools. Daycare, once a luxury of the upper classes, has become a working-class necessity, and can easily cost between $6,000 and $16,000 per year. And with the dearth of well-paying jobs and the collapse of a highly-paid blue-collar work force, college is increasingly seen not as an option or a luxury but as a basic necessity for future survival at a standard of living above that of a trailer park.

The AP article concludes with Segal's observation: "We find a society in which long-standing, legitimate need is widely unmet, and which in some instances is more thoroughly unmet than in previous, less affluent generations."

One of the nation's more insightful folk philosophers, Tim Underwood, noted (upon reading the above): "Economically speaking, things have been going down hill from the 'hay days' of the late 1950s and early-to mid-1960s when dad supported the family and mom could stay home. Economically we'll never have it that easy again. They didn't work nearly as long or as hard, to support their standard of living.

"But that generation of Americans had it easy at the expense of the third world, even more so than is true today. In part this was because the resources that American corporations were stripping from the Earth domestically and abroad, such as wood and oil and especially minerals, were still relatively plentiful. As consumers we all share the blame for the damage inflicted by this ongoing devouring mechanism. This process also tends to feed wealth into the western world's consumer societies, and especially into the richest one to two percent of the population.

"Now, as the world's natural resources are becoming exhausted, this stripping is going on in new and different ways. Middle class Americans are currently being divested of their security, their jobs, their disposable income, the quality of their family life and their free time—as corporations 'downsize' and become more 'efficient.'

"The endemic American free-floating anxiety and malaise is in small part end-of-millennium angst, and in large part a consequence of our loss of security. America of the 1950s suffered from fear of the Atom Bomb and fear of Russia (our national shadow). Now Americans dread the future because unlike our parents we can no longer envision a brighter tomorrow. What we *can* see are overpopulation and environmental degradation. Things are getting worse. If you *know* things are going to be worse next year and worse in ten years and worse for your kids and you feel helpless to turn this around, wouldn't that make you anxious? Despite fear of the Bomb and paranoia, in the 1950s Americans lived with a very rosy picture of the future: "Better Living Through Chemistry." Things had been getting better and were apparently going to continue to get better. People will sacrifice and put up with a lot, if they have that certainty."

So we have this theory, this possibility, that some of what we call ADD is actually the product of children and adults living lives saturated with anxiety, producing stress, producing physical, mental, and emotional changes in us. But is there any objective evidence of this?

Yes, says the Gallup organization, America's most famous and most credible polling company. In a survey conducted in late 1995, they found that while 13% of adult Americans had reported trouble sleeping in 1991, nearly half of all Americans reported trouble sleeping just four years later in 1995. This more-than-quadrupling of the number of people experiencing sleep problems is caused, according to the National Sleep Foundation, by the "increasingly frantic pace of life in the '90s, along with work pressures."

And this isn't just an isolated or irrelevant phenomena: one third of the respondents had fallen asleep while driving and ten percent reported that this had led to an automobile accident.

The Gallup poll, with only an error margin of plus or minus three percentage points, found that Americans not only are experiencing more stress in their daily lives, but also that stress is measurable in an epidemic of sleep disorders.

Lack of sleep is another condition shown to have an effect on a person's attention span.

So the concept that at least some of what we call ADD is caused by our modern society "going to hell in a hand-basket," as one ADD adult described it to me at a recent conference, may be more than just an odd possibility.

Solutions

Possible solutions to this problem would include getting more sleep, finding less stressful jobs or places to live, and trying in general to reduce stress levels in life. Learning meditation, for example, has been shown to be effective in improving emotional well-being. Similarly, many people find that moving to the country or finding a new job serve to transform their lives in a positive way.

As Americans become more and more nervous about their economic future, it's becoming fashionable to live a simpler life— using recycled materials, shopping in thrift stores, eating less extravagantly, and driving a more humble automobile. These lifestyle changes appear to be very healthy overall, and people experiencing stress in their lives may want to consider some of them.

We're Living in the Last Days and the World's About To End

"As to the changes physical again: The earth will be broken up in the western portion of America. The greater portion of Japan must go into the sea. The upper portion of Europe will be changed as in the twinkling of an eye. Land will appear off the east coast of America. There will be upheavals in the Arctic and in the Antarctic that will make for the eruption of volcanoes in the Torrid areas, and there will be the shifting then of the poles... And these will begin in those periods in '58 to '98..."
— Edgar Cayce, reading 3976-15

My son Justin is, in many ways, one of the wisest people I know.

One night he and I were driving around downtown Atlanta, looking for an Ethiopian restaurant he was pretty sure existed, but couldn't remember where. It gave us an hour or so to talk.

"You know the end of the world is coming, don't you, Dad?" he said.

"I've heard that, but they've been saying it for thousands of years," I said.

"I think this time it's real," he said. "The ozone hole is getting huge, the country is bankrupt and so now I'm in debt and I'm only seventeen, the world only has a 40-year oil supply left, there are bombs and terrorists everywhere, there are too many people to feed, and it says in the Bible that the Apocalypse is coming."

"What do your friends think of this?" I said.

"Everybody agrees. It's gonna happen in our lifetimes.

Probably before or just after the year 2000. Did you know that there are six letters in each of Ronald Wilson Reagan's names? He set it up. Everybody knows it."

"Everybody?"

"Everybody I know. At least everybody who thinks at all about anything. The stupid kids just want to play football, you know? But anybody who thinks about the state of the world even for five minutes has to know how inevitable this is."

"What are people doing about it?" I said.

He shrugged and spread his fingers out on his knees. "What can we do? We weren't around to stop Reagan from running up the national debt. We have no say in the wars that they'll send us off to fight. We can't stop people from having too many babies."

"So what do your friends do with and about this knowledge?"

"Have fun. Party. Why bother with anything else?"

Why, indeed.

The history of the year 1000 in Europe is fascinating. In the years leading up to the millennial change, people seemed to go nuts. They left their families and adultery was rampant. Crime escalated to the point where many local governments completely broke down. Religious cults exploded, often led by renegade monks, and many people sold everything they owned to join these groups who expected to be taken to heaven on the first day of the year 1000 in the Rapture. In the year 999, individual and mass suicides were commonplace, as Europe approached a final frenzy of expectation and fear about the end of the old millennium. This continued through much of the year 1000, and it wasn't until 1001 that things began to return to what then was considered normal.

Today, it's hard for any teenager to flip through the channels on their cable system and not find at least one televangelist preaching the battle of Armageddon between pitches for money.

In addition to the biblical prophecies that most people are familiar with, the prophecies of Nostradamus are also widely circulating these days. There's a news group dedicated to them on the Internet, and, oddly enough, the writings of this man living in the year 1555, before America was even colonized, are a popular subject of discussion among contemporary high school students.

Nostradamus' Predictions

Nostradamus predicted the rise of Napoleon and Hitler—naming both—before either was born. This, of course, did wonders for his credibility in the eyes of contemporary people. He also predicted that in the "new land of Ameriga" three brothers would come to power, and two would be cut down in their prime, altering the future of a nation that didn't exist at the time Nostradamus lived.

When Nostradamus wrote the following, many people became concerned. He named a specific year, which he rarely did, using the phrase "Mars will reign" which he always used as a metaphor for war (Mars was the Roman god of war), and specified the battle of Armageddon (d'Angolmois in his native French).

The year 1999, seventh month,
A great king of terror will descent from the skies,
To resuscitate the great king of Angolmois,
Around this time Mars will reign for the good cause.

And this other reference to a country which did not yet exist, and an odd mention of possibly a southerner (Reb):

There will be a head of London from the government of Americha,
The Island of Scotland, he will pave you with ice;
They will have Reb for King, a very false Antichrist,
Who will put them all in an uproar.

And:
The third Antichrist, soon annihilated,
But his bloody war will last 27 years.

In addition to all the biblical prophecies, and the words of Nostradamus (recited on TV by no less than Orson Wells), there are also the gloom-and-doom words of contemporary music, much of which centers around the breakdown of institutions and even the metaphysical reasons for the destruction of the earth. Musicians from Al Stewart to Bob Dylan to Bob Marley to the punk-rock group Bad Religion have written and performed major-hit songs about the battle of Armageddon or the end of the world.

Modern children are awash in a sea of negativism and paranoia that's perhaps unprecedented in American history. Particularly in the religious arena, heroes have been toppled or have made fools of themselves (Swaggart, Bakker, Roberts), or are seen by some as having sold out for political power and media big-bucks (Robertson, Falwell). Popular culture is drenched in the idea, with movies like *The Hot Zone*, *The Andromeda Strain*, and the best-selling book *The Coming Plague*. The killer and incurable disease of AIDS is running rampant through our population, now reaching close to plague proportions, with young people being the fastest-growing victim-group. The media is almost daily filled with stories portending end-of-the-world scenarios, from the collapse of the American government to the destruction of endangered species to the disintegration of the ozone layer. Not to mention wars, famines, nuclear meltdowns, toxic-waste spills, and revolutions all over the earth.

All this can increase the percentage of young people being diagnosed with ADD in two ways.

First, numerous studies have shown that when people are under stress they're less able to concentrate, they become more distractible and impulsive, and, if the stress is sufficiently severe and long-lasting, they will begin to engage in self-destructive behaviors. Studies from the last century have shown this to be true of animals ranging from rats to lemmings, and recent work on humans shows the same pattern.

Second, one of the most common reasons why children are referred for an ADD diagnosis is that they're failing in school. And, ADD or not, if you don't think the world is going to last for more than the next few years, why bother trying to succeed in school? For many of these kids, "Don't Worry, Be Happy" has become the slogan of the day. Their parents' fears about future income potential, or finding the right college or career seem distant and hollow, and perhaps even naive, given the "secret" knowledge they have that it's all pointless anyway.

Another way of looking at this was presented to me during a speech I gave on ADD in Laguna Beach, California. I had just talked about the experience I'd chronicled in *ADD Success Stories* of being in India and having an Indian physician tell me that, as a Hindu, he considered people with ADD to be "old souls." I then joked that I should have moved to India years ago.

But during the Q&A period, a woman who took the comment quite seriously asked from the audience, "Do you think it's possible that we're actually in the end times and that more of these old souls are incarnating now because they're going to be needed to handle all the changes coming with the end of the old and the beginning of the new age?"

It being California, nobody in the audience laughed; I was confronted with about 150 serious, anticipating faces. So I answered truthfully (in my own personal truth): "I don't know, but I certainly wouldn't discard that as a possibility."

Solutions

The current situation in the world, and the end of the millennium, provide us with an opportunity for spiritual self-examination and growth. More and more people are rejecting the materialism and greed of the 1980s, looking for ways to live that are more compatible with the needs of the earth, and searching for answers to spiritual questions.

Those of us alive during this time are presented with a wonderful opportunity to use the tension, angst, and oddity of a millennial change to examine and explore spiritual options. This is something that happens only once every thirty generations. Rather than viewing it as a threat, we should rejoice in the opportunity to live through a time that others in history have only been able to dream about.

There Are Too Many People

"Hell is a city much like London—A populous and smoky city."

—Peter Bell the Third, 1819

Our newspapers are filled with reports of the explosion of violence in modern society, from the genocide of the Khmer Rouge to the slaughter of civilians in Bosnia to the violence in America's inner cities.

On a more local level, teachers complain that they're identifying ever greater numbers of ADD/ADHD children, and that today's ADD/ADHD children are more likely now than 20 years ago to act out in a violent or antisocial fashion. Suicide among young people has tripled in the last 30 years and is now the third leading cause of death of those between the ages of 15 and 24. Many theories are put forth to explain this, usually having to do with the breakdown of the nuclear family, the pervasiveness of violence in popular media, and the success or failure of particular political approaches to solving society's ills.

But what if changes in the cultural level of violence are genetic? What if the drive for aggression is built into us, triggered whenever the ratio between population and available resources hit a certain threshold. Perhaps this trigger-point is different for people in/from hunting or farming societies? Farming societies, after all, generally have a much higher population density; it would make sense, therefore, that they'd have a much higher tolerance for high population density.

Consider the Tiger Grand Canyon Salamander. This animal is

generally very docile, and, when there is an ample food supply, would never think of attacking its own species. When water and food are scarce, however, this little animal actually grows a larger head, a whole new set of sharp teeth, and begins to actively seek out its own kind to eat. The stronger and most quickly-mutated salamanders will eat the smaller and less-quick to mutate ones until the ratio of food-and-water to salamanders reaches some genetically-determined point. The survivors then lose their teeth and their heads return to normal size.

Similarly, most people are familiar with the legendary behavior of lemmings, who, when their population density reaches a certain critical mass, commit mass suicide. And students of psychology are familiar with studies of crowding among rats. When the population density hits a certain point, adult rats will begin to cannibalize their young, using the rat pups for food. They'll also begin a whole series of violent antisocial behaviors which are uncommon in non-population-stressed rat communities.

In an article in a recent issue of *Current Health* magazine, Sandra Arbetter M.S.W. points out that poverty, alcohol, or even abuse can trigger changes in the balance of serotonin and noradrenaline in the human brain. In these situations, the noradrenaline levels will increase (this is one of the hormones involved in the fight-and-flight response), whereas the "thinking" neurotransmitter, serotonin, will decrease. She notes that people suffering from an imbalance of these neurotransmitters—caused by violence and overcrowding in our society—"need a lot of outside stimulation to feel alive," and goes on to suggest that they may even resort to criminality or violence to get that stimulation.

It's interesting to note how a researcher approaching the issue from an entirely different viewpoint, looking purely at aggression would conclude with the same note about the need to feel aliveness.

Solutions

It's possible that we're seeing more ADD because children and adults with ADD are more likely to impulsively express their aggressive feelings. This baseline of aggression could be the result of too many people and too few resources in the world.

The solutions to this situation are twofold. For the long view, of course, we'd want to work to help people have fewer children worldwide, and also to develop the resources to nourish the humans alive on planet Earth now.

Over the short term, many people returning to rural areas are finding that their lives become far less stressful as a result.

CHAPTER SIX

Brain Chemistry and Physiology

Some researchers and clinicians report that the right frontal lobe of the brains of "normal" people is larger than that of people with ADD, whose left and right frontal lobes are of roughly the same size. Is it because these "normal" people knuckled down at an early age and practiced "being inhibited" (the theorized function of this lobe)? That like a weight lifter who works out only one arm, and has a huge right but skinny left bicep, they're somehow mentally out of balance and therefore highly inhibited? Or is this the way humans are supposed to be, and those with ADD just haven't yet caught up?

And what about the notion that the brain—an organ just like any other—may react to irritations ranging from the physical to the chemical with responses which we call ADD-like behavior? Or that, as I've often said in my speeches over the years, is testosterone really the most dangerous drug in the world and drives some of what we call hyperactivity and ADD?

This chapter examines these questions, as well as looking at one particularly dangerous instance when a diagnosis of ADD can be life-threatening.

Brain Irritations

"The smallest sensation of pain may excite rebellious dispositions in the mind..."
— Madame De Stael, *Holstein Reflections on Suicide*

Could one cause of what we call ADD or ADDH be an irritation of the central nervous system?

Ben Feingold, a pediatric allergist with Kaiser-Permanente in San Francisco, was an early proponent of this theory, although an Atlanta chiropractor has developed an interesting variation on it.

Feingold first came up with his idea when he was treating children with severe, unexplained skin rashes. He discovered many of his young patients were allergic to specific food substances, more often than not the food flavorings and colorings derived from coal tar known as salicylates. Aspirin belongs to the same family of compounds, and many of these children were also sensitive to aspirin.

Having found dozens of children with this sensitivity, Feingold developed a diet that was free of salicylates and put his young skin-rash patients on it. What happened next caught him by surprise, however: the families of these children reported that the kids, when they went on the diet, not only lost their skin rashes but also no longer exhibited hyperactive behavior.

Feingold replicated this many times over the years, and finally concluded that if a food allergy was severe enough to cause the skin to erupt, it must also be strong enough to irritate the central nervous system, causing a metaphorical "rash on the brain."

Having proved this to his own satisfaction, and that of many of the other pediatricians and allergists with whom he worked, he took a next step which was largely a leap of logic and faith. If this food allergy was causing hyperactive behavior in his patients with skin disorders, might it not be possible that it was causing the same problem among those hyperactive children who didn't have sensitive skin?

What he and subsequent researchers found out is that for a small but measurable subset of the population, this appears to be true. When I was executive director of a residential treatment facility for children in the late 1970s and early 1980s, we experimented with the Feingold diet, and found one child who was clearly responsive to it. Others seemed not to be food-sensitive, or at least not to the foods we'd eliminated with the Feingold diet. I published the results of this study in *The Journal of Orthomolecular Psychiatry*.

A variation on this theme was suggested recently by Atlanta chiropractor Beth Bradford. Dr. Bradford showed me the case histories of numerous children who had come into her practice with the diagnosis of hyperactivity or ADD/ADDH, most of them on stimulant medications.

"The odd thing that I noticed after seeing many of these children," she commented, "was that they all had subluxations (misalignments of the spinal vertebrae) in the same region: that of the upper cervical (top of the neck) area."

We went through a large pile of charts and sets of X-rays as Dr. Bradford showed me case after case of hyperactive children who'd calmed down as the result of her chiropractic adjustments. All but one of the cases she showed me, in fact, were children who had been able to discontinue taking drugs for their ADD. She said other chiropractors had reported similar results to her and in the literature of the profession.

The mechanism of this is relatively simple. The spinal cord, which passes out of the skull at the area of the occiput and down into and through the spine, is a long and thick bundle of nerves which provides the ability for motion to the entire body. It's both sturdy and fragile. If it's injured (as happened to actor Christopher Reeves recently when he fell off a horse), paralysis of the entire body can result. On the other hand, the spinal cord is tough enough to flex as the head is moved from side to side or twisted in the course of normal exercise.

Where Dr. Bradford believes this ties into ADD is where the brain stem connects the spinal cord to the brain. She believes that vertebral subluxation complex can put direct pressure on the brain stem and spinal cord, which will disrupt signals from the brain being sent to the rest of the body via the brain stem and spinal cord. Dr. Bradford's theory speculates that if there's a spinal misalignment of the upper neck that's drastic enough to stretch or pull on the spinal cord, it could cause a mechanical action that would, like Dr. Feingold's food additives, "irritate" the brain itself. This would sometimes lead to behaviors that we'd call hyperactive.

And Dr. Bradford is not alone in that opinion.

In the classic *Textbook of Clinical Chiropractic*, several studies are referenced tieing chiropractic care to amelioration of ADD or hyperactivity. In the *Journal of Manipulative Physiological Therapy* one researcher showed significant improvement of ADD children when chiropractic adjustments were used. Another study specifically targeted the neck area as being involved in ADD and hyperactivity. Marilyn Lalka, an Atlanta chiropractor, provided me with literally dozens of studies, a videotape, and case histories which corroborated what Dr. Bradford had shared with me. I also was introduced to another Atlanta chiropractor who specializes in ADD and spends virtually all of his attentions on this upper-spine area.

So here we have another possible contributor to the epidemic of ADD diagnoses in the United States: irritation of the brain, both chemical and mechanical.

Solutions

Chiropractic is generally safe when done by a competent professional, and not particularly expensive. It's also covered by some insurance plans. I prefer not to have X-rays taken that some chiropractors insist on and you can generally find one who'll work on you or your child without the X-rays. The technique itself is, at worst, physically therapeutic, and at best may help alleviate some symptoms of hyperactivity.

Similarly, there may be some children reactive to salicylates, who would benefit from an elimination diet. A recent article in the Atlanta newspapers pointed out that at least one researcher thought perhaps the steady decline in heart attacks among the U.S. population over the past 20 years might be a result of the increasing amounts of salicylates in our food, as a result of all the artificial colors and flavors. The article, while never mentioning Feingold's work, talked in glowing terms about the fact that the average American consumes between 50 and 100 milligrams of salicylate-containing food additives a day(!). Since these compounds are so closely related to aspirin, which is known to reduce heart attacks when taken daily, although the side effects of stomach bleeding and fatal strokes are a cause for worry, this may account for the decline in heart attacks. But it may also be causing some children to have behavioral problems.

Sugar and Sugary Foods Alter Brain Chemistry

"Sweets are delicious. But eat too many sweets and they become too much, or there becomes too much of you."
—Rob Kall

Considerable press attention was given in 1995 to a study in which a group of hyperactive children was given sugar or Nutra-Sweet to try to determine if the sugar was causing their hyperactivity. While it seemed like a good control from a physiological point of view to give children identical candy, many in the ADD community were highly critical of the study.

Mainly, it didn't account for the way the brain reacts to stimuli to which it's become conditioned. Pavlov proved in the last century that if a bell was rung at the same time a dog was fed, after a period of time the dog would automatically start to salivate when a bell was rung, even if no food was present. Thousands of studies since that time have proven that the body and brain don't need a "primary" stimulus (such as the food, in that case) to provoke a neurological response. A conditioned response can be evoked by an associated stimulus.

The brain has become used to going wild in response to sugar, for example, and there's a neurochemical or biological basis to that. The "bell" for the brain, though, is the sweet taste. It was illogical to think that providing the sweet taste without sugar wouldn't still trigger a brain response. The brain senses the NutraSweet, assumes it's sugar, and begins the process of response. And that's just what the study found, in fact: hyperactive kids are still hyperactive when given either sugar or Nutra-

Sweet. Nonetheless, the sugar industry and the press were quick to jump on that study and claim that it "proved" that sugar doesn't contribute to hyperactivity, when, of course, it did nothing of the sort.

Less press attention was given to a study which was not funded by the sugar industry or any sugary-food manufacturers and was published in the journal in 1995.*Pediatric Research* The study, titled "Blunted catecholamine responses after glucose ingestion in children with attention deficit disorder," actually measured the brain chemistry responses of two groups of children, one ADD and the other "normal." What they found was startling.

The children were challenged with a dose of glucose which is pretty standard for testing for hypoglycemia, that being 1.75 grams of sugar for each kilogram of body weight. There were 17 ADD children and 11 control children, all with identical glucose and insulin levels. These researchers, however, were far more thorough than those who did the earlier study mentioned; they also measured the levels of epinephrine and norepinephrine in the blood of the children. These are two hormonal neurotransmitters intimately involved with the flight-or-fight response and which control levels of physical activity. Epinephrine is closely related to the active ingredient in the antihistamine Sudafed, for example, which will produce nervous and hyperactive behavior in most people if it's taken in large doses. Norepinephrine, on the other hand, is associated with a calming response.

Three and five hours after giving the ADD and the control-group children their dose of sugar, their blood was tested for these compounds. It was found that the excitation-increasing epinephrine levels rose at a "significantly greater" rate in the ADD children than in the control group, while the calming norepinephrine levels *fell* in the ADD children, but not in the control group. There were differences in the levels of both of these compounds between the ADD and control-group children as a result of the administration of the sugar. The ADD children's levels of the activity-increased neurotransmitter increasing, while the calming neurotransmitter fell. For these ADD kids, this represents a double-whammy.

Solutions

The researchers in this study, while pointing out that it wasn't positively conclusive because of the small group studied, suggested that until more research is done in this area parents of ADD children might want to consider restricting their children's sugar intake. (It may be a while before more research is done in this area because much of university research these days is corporate-funded by companies with an interest in selling sugar-based products.)

Dysfunctional or Underdeveloped Frontal Brain Lobes

There are three different kinds of brains, the one under-stands things unassisted, the other understands things when shown by others, and the third understands neither alone nor with the explanations of others. The first kind is most excellent, the second kind also excellent, but the third useless.
— Machiavelli, Niccolo, *The Prince*

Dr. Judith Rapoport, chief of the Child Psychiatry Branch at the National Institute of Mental Health in Bethesda, Maryland, reported in *Attention!* magazine on research she and her colleagues had done using a hugely expensive machine that images the inside of the brain without using radiation. Nuclear Magnetic Resonance (NMR) allows a researcher to see actual brain structures, without having to inject a person with radioactive dyes, such as are used in PET and SPECT scans. They can therefore be used on children without the ethical and medical concerns associated with irradiation.

Using the NMR machinery, Dr. Rapoport's team found physical differences in brain structures between ADD and non-ADD children. Specifically, they found that in non-ADD children the right frontal lobe of the brain is slightly larger than the left frontal lobe, whereas in ADD children the right frontal lobe is about the same size.

Current neurobiological thought puts inhibition types of behaviors in the right frontal lobe, so if a lower threshold for inhibition is characteristic of ADD, it's not surprising, according to Dr. Rapoport, that this part of the brain would be under-developed.

This also falls in line with the observation I first published in 1993: people with ADD have a different perception of the passage of time and a different sense of time from non-ADD people. Instead of time flowing in a linear and predictable fashion, for people with ADD it often seems to be either rushing (when they're on-task and excited about something) or moving excruciatingly slowly (when they're bored or awaiting gratification). For people with ADD there seem to be only two times: "now" and "some other time." This distorted sense of time, I theorized back then, would lead to impulsive behavior, often even self-destructive impulsivity. The ADD person doesn't have a solid enough sense of past and future to easily learn lessons from the past or to project the possibly painful consequences of his actions into the future.

A few decades ago it was discovered that our frontal lobes are where we experience time and why all other mammals, none of which have frontal lobes, live only in an eternal "now." This would also tie into Dr. Rapoport's finding that the frontal lobes of ADD people may be less functional than those of non-ADD people.

But if this explains the mechanism of ADD, how does this difference in brains come about?

Certainly there is evidence of a genetic component in ADD. However, in studies of identical twins where one has ADD, only 51% of the twin's siblings also had ADD. While that's statistically much better than the 34% concurrence among fraternal twins, and strongly suggests at least a genetic predisposition or weakness toward ADD, it also shows that genetics aren't the one and only reason for ADD.

In the *Attention!* interview, Dr. Rapoport talks about looking forward to examining the brains of twins with ADD, speculating that "if it's correct that ADD is related to some sort of non-genetic developmental influence then it could open up another line of research."

Given how plastic and subject to physical modification the brain is in early childhood, it may well be that many of the theories in this book of why we have ADD relate to mechanisms involving the frontal lobes. They may cause the right frontal lobe to either develop identically to the left one, or to grow to a slightly larger size as we see in "normal" people. It may also explain how certain types of behavior modification and exercises like EEG Neurofeedback, which can increase blood-flow and general activity in specific parts of the brain, can have a therapeutic effect on individuals with ADD.

Solutions

Given how plastic young brains are (and even adult brains are), it makes sense that exercises that help the frontal lobes to work more efficiently may be useful for people with ADD. These exercises may range from highly-disciplined activities such as learning martial arts, to EEG Neurofeedback.

ADD as a Variation of Normal Male Behavior

"I have always lived violently, drunk hugely, eaten too much or not at all, slept around the clock or missed two nights of sleeping, worked too hard and too long in glory, or slobbed for a time in utter laziness. I've lifted, pulled, chopped, climbed, made love with joy and taken my hangovers as a consequence not as a punishment. I did not want to surrender fierceness for a small gain in yardage."
—John Steinbeck, *Travels With Charlie*, 1962

Although it's politically incorrect to say so, men and women, and boys and girls, are different. The extent of these differences have been observed since the beginning of human history, most obviously in the physical realm. And literature dating back 5,000 years shows observations about different thinking styles between men and women.

But how different? And could it be that some of what's called ADD is really just a boy-child behaving as he's been programmed by evolution, in a classroom with a woman-teacher who has little compassion for behaviors she can't understand?

These gender differences have been the object of some very detailed studies recently, the most notable by Dr. Ruben C. Gur, director of the brain behavior laboratory at the University of Pennsylvania. In a recent interview with the Associated Press, he pointed out that the most "striking difference" between men and women is how each deals with emotions and emotional situations.

Using sophisticated PET scanners to peer into the brains of men and women, Dr. Gur and his colleagues found that women's brains have greater neurochemical activity than do men's in the areas that control symbolic emotional responses. This difference shows up in the following ways, the researchers found:

❖ Because of physical/neurological brain differences, men and women have different cognitive abilities, including those of judgment and memory. Men are better at visualizing an object in space, rotating it in their minds and seeing it from several different angles; women are better at more abstract mental tasks such as sorting things by a particular criteria such as size, color, or shape.

❖ Women are better able to remember things presented to them verbally than are men. Since most of our modern-day schoolwork is presented verbally, this may account for why so many boys have difficulty in learning or need more visually-presented information for learning to take place.

❖ Men have higher limbic system activity—that part of the brain often called the "reptilian brain." This produces instantaneous flight-or-fight responses and other seemingly emotional responses which happen very fast with no opportunity for thought or conscious control. Women, on the other hand, have great neurobiological activity in the cingulate gyrus, thought to be one of the more "recently evolved" portions of the human brain which deals with refined and symbolic emotional expression. This gives women a huge advantage over men in looking at the face of another person and "reading" their emotions. The inherent inability of men to do this may contribute to their being perceived as oppositional, defiant, or thoughtless. Instead, it simply may be that they're missing the emotional cues of the other person.

While all this new research certainly doesn't mean that ADD is a "guy thing," or that it's a "myth," it may help explain why ADD seems so much more prevalent—and is more frequently diagnosed—in boys and men than in girls and women.

Solutions

Instead of viewing a child in a vacuum, let's look at his or her behavior in a more general context. Include in this overview the teacher, other children, the cultural milieu, the classroom, and the family. And in each instance, let's look at the messages about gender which are being given to the child, particularly to little boys, and try to teach them how to observe other's emotions, and to be more of a cooperator and less of a dominator.

ADD is Not Just One Thing

"As usual with the exploration of complex subjects, there are more questions here than answers. And there are dangers too."

—Bill Moyers, *Healing & The Mind*

Susan knows she's ADD because her home is a mess. "If I can't see it, it doesn't exist," she says, so therefore "everything important or that I need to remember is out visible someplace, usually in a pile." The result is what some people would call chaos, although Susan says she has to have it this way. "When I tried filing things, I'd invariably lose them forever."

Bill, a high school student, has no problem with filing things. His desk at school and his homework area at home are both spotless, and, in fact, he has what he describes as a "superstition" that he can't do his schoolwork until the work area he's in is clean and tidy. He's highly distractible, however: the slightest noise, the most insignificant motion, even a stray thought will sent him off on a daydreaming thought-train that may take him twenty minutes to recover from.

Jack doesn't have much of a problem with organization or distractibility, although he admits that both represent a constant challenge. His issue is his hyperactivity; he can't stop moving or talking. "I'm always on the go," he told me as he was about to leave home for a trip to Europe. "If I'm not traveling, I'm talking. If I'm not talking, I'm working on something. I can't stand to be bored."

Donna, a psychiatric nurse, knew she was ADD because the other doctors and nurses she worked with often asked her if she was on drugs (she wasn't). "I'd just get spacey, you know? I'd walk from one room to another to get something, and before I even arrived in the second room, I'd already forgotten why I was heading there."

And the mother of Jared, age five, knew her pediatrician's diagnosis of ADD was correct when he pointed out that Jared was always jumping into risky activities. "He's run out into traffic, jumped off tables, tried to climb up to the roof of the house, and even tried to start the car once when he found my husband's keys," his mom said. "He has to be ADD; he's an incredible risk-taker."

Jared, Donna, Jack, Bill, and Susan are all certain they have Attention Deficit Disorder. All tried Ritalin or Dexedrine and reported that it helped or solved their problem. Yet each, if confronted with the other, would probably say, "I'm not like that person."

ADD is a tough diagnosis or category to get your arms around. With over a dozen "questions" in the DSM criteria, and some (such as that proposed by Hallowell & Ratey in their book *Driven To Distraction*) running as long as 20 to 50 questions, a lot of room for individual variations exists.

There's also no definitive market or test for ADD, at least as of this writing. No gene has been definitely identified, no blood or saliva test clearly shows that a person has ADD, and no physical characteristics lead to a positive diagnosis.

So what if ADD were actually a catch-all category for a half-dozen or more completely different conditions? And, even more heretical, what if many of those conditions don't really represent identifiable pathologies, but are merely aspects of the human condition?

For example, scientists who study the difference between brain structures and behavior point out that certain behaviors can probably be associated with certain types of brains and brain chemistries. When particular structures are weak, loosely connected, or simply operate at a different-from-normal threshold, those differences will manifest as specific and often-predictable behavior profiles. For example; an ADD person might exhibit these tendencies:

❖ **Thalamus/Recticular Activating System (which con-
trols our level of overall brain arousal)**
—Inability to stay on task
—Easily distracted, often leading to mental errors in logic
—A craving for large amounts of stimulation

❖ **Frontal Lobes (which provide our sense of orderliness
and our ability to measure, sense, and live in time)**
—Lacks impulse control so makes impulsive decisions
—Hyperactive
—Disorganized
—Wild mood swings and high emotional intensity
—May be stubborn, defiant, oppositional

❖ **Parietal Lobe (where speech, language, and certain
types of thought are processed)**
—Wanders off into daydreaming easily: may even spend most of
life in this state
—Internally distractible: distracted by their own thoughts
—Specific Learning Disabilities, especially disorders of visual
processing, mathematical processing, and prosody.

❖ **Specific Sensory Areas (visual or auditory cortex, for
example, where sight or sound are processed)**
—Easily distracted only by the type of sense affected

❖ **Limbic System (the "reptilian brain" in which primi-
tive/baseline functions are moderated, such as appetite, fight-
or-flight, sexual desire, etc.)**
—Appears either under-or over-motivated
—New stimuli in the environment elicit unpredictable responses
(or sometimes even no response)
—Sometimes over-responds to seemingly irrelevant or inconse-
quential things

Any of these variations in the human brain could produce
behaviors which may be clinically defined as attention deficit
disorder. Yet each is different in its cause, its effect, and even in
the appropriate interventions (medication, strategy-training, etc.)
that may be effective for it.

The waters are further muddied by recent research done at the Washington University School of Medicine in St. Louis and Sarah Herzog Memorial Hospital in Jerusalem. It began when Dr. C. Robert Cloninger of Washington University advanced the theory that four primary and independent personality traits account for much of the vast range of visible human behavior: *novelty seeking, harm avoidance, reward dependence,* and *persistence.* Cloninger went a step further than mere psychology, however, when he proposed that all of these behaviors were neurochemically mediated, and suggested that with novelty-seeking behavior the neurotransmitter involved was probably dopamine.

Dr. Richard P. Ebstein and associates at the Sarah Herzog Memorial Hospital picked up the gauntlet of that challenge, and administered a personality questionnaire to 124 individuals in Jerusalem, a mixture of Sephardic and Ashkenazi Jews. The questionnaire was designed to determine each person's level of novelty-seeking behavior. Simultaneous with that, Ebstein drew blood from the volunteers and looked at the D4DR gene, which is known to regulate the formation of one class of dopamine receptors in the brain.

What they found was that the higher the individual scored on the novelty-seeking-behavior questionnaire, the physically longer and more complex was their D4DR gene. This study was followed up by Dr. Jonathan Benjamin of the National Institutes of Mental Health in Bethesda, Md., with 315 people, many of them pairs of male siblings. The results were similar: the longer the D4DR gene, the more novelty-seeking behavior the individuals exhibited.

This is much more fundamental, visceral, and narrowly-focused than ADD, but in the wake of this research being published many psychologists and ADD experts are asking out loud to what extent this clearly-genetic novelty-seeking behavior and an ADD diagnosis may go hand-in-glove.

Perhaps so much ADD is being diagnosed now for the same reason a hundred years ago many people were diagnosed with "excess blood" and were bled to relieve virtually feverous, nauseated, or diarrheal conditions: Our diagnostic criteria is blurry.

Solutions

Keep an open mind to the various conditions or behaviors that may contribute to, or look like, ADD. Continue to learn and grow, and think twice before dropping life's problems into one neat little diagnostic category which may actually be far less well-defined than many people think.

Some "ADD" May Really Be
Undiagnosed Thyroid Disorders

*"Normally, we do not so much look at things as overlook
them."* —Alan Watts

The thyroid gland, located in the neck just behind and around the larynx, is one of the master organs in the body. It produces hormones which trigger other parts of the endocrine system to regulate our body temperature, level of arousal, and even our digestive processes. When it's not functioning properly, it can have a profound effect on a person's emotional states, short-term memory, and even on the body's ability to fight off infection.

It's the opinion of some experts in the field of endocrinology that some of what is being diagnosed as ADD, particularly in adults, is really thyroid dysfunction. Broda Barnes, M.D., in his book *Hypothyroidism: The Unsuspected Illness* gives an example of this problem in a child whose apparent hyperactivity and ADD was determined to be actually the result of low thyroid function. When the hormones were appropriately balanced, the child became "normal."

Several books and articles recently published purport to detail the "unique" ways that ADD shows up in women. One woman I know read one of these books and concluded that she must have ADD, because she drank eight cups of coffee a day, was often tired, and had poor follow-through in many areas of her life. She tried Ritalin and found that it perked her up, and this further caused her to conclude that she had ADD.

When she went to the doctor, however, because she was experiencing recurrent infections and intestinal problems, he noticed her low body temperature and took a blood sample to measure her levels of thyroid-produced hormones. "They were so low the doctor was amazed I was still alive," she said. The doctor put her on a synthetic thyroid hormone supplement to bring her thyroid levels back up to normal, and most of her supposed ADD symptoms began to vanish, along with her need for either Ritalin or huge quantities of coffee.

Dr. Barnes says in his book that hypothyroidism is far more widespread than most people—and even most physicians—realize, because it can masquerade as so many different conditions. He speculates that it may affect as many as forty percent of all Americans, afflicting far more women than men. This is perhaps because of depletion of the essential iodine for the thyroid by a growing fetus during pregnancy, or perhaps because menstruation depletes the body of small amounts of iodine along with the blood.

Additionally, large areas of the United States have soil that is notoriously iodine deficient (the Midwest, for example). Here there seem to be large numbers of people, particularly women, who have often-undiagnosed hypothyroidism. And our factory farming systems, with their dependence on synthetic fertilizers which replace only a small fraction of the nutrients depleted from the soil, make the problem even worse. Levels of iodine and other nutrients essential to the thyroid and endocrine system in supermarket foods nationwide may be dramatically lower than those found before the advent of chemical fertilizers.

Unfortunately, if a woman with hypothyroidism were to go on stimulant medication therapy instead of on thyroid-replacement therapy, her "ADD" would seem to get better. But her overall health would become at grave risk, as the body's systems, particularly the immune system, would continue to deteriorate from the lack of thyroid hormone.

Dr. Barnes and others would advise a person suspecting ADD, particularly with fatigue or hyperactivity, to first rule out thyroid dysfunction. The test is easy and inexpensive, and can be performed by any doctor with access to a nearby laboratory.

Solutions

If you suspect that you have a thyroid or other endocrine disorder, see your physician or an endocrinologist immediately. The blood test is simple, relatively painless, and inexpensive; it could literally save your life if this turns out to be your problem.

CHAPTER SEVEN

Contemporary Lifestyles and Habits

Adolf Hitler, in *Mein Kampf*, identified three types of people. He felt two groups would be useful for the Nazi party: those "who believe everything they read," and those who "no longer believe anything" but could be indoctrinated. The third group he considered dangerous. They were singled out early on for persecution in the Third Reich. This group, Hitler wrote, must be destroyed because they are those who "think independently, who try to form a judgment of their own about everything, and who submit most thoroughly everything they have been told to an examination and further thought of their own."

Hitler's Deputy, Rudolph Hess, said in 1984: "It was constantly impressed upon me in forceful terms that I must obey promptly the wishes and commands of my parents, teachers and priests, and indeed of all grown-up people including servants, and that nothing must distract me from this duty. Whatever they said was always right. These basic principles by which I was brought up became second nature to me."

In this chapter we look at some of the things in our culture and lifestyles—from television advertising to short attention spans to sunlight starvation to an educational culture which would have loved Rudolph Hess—as playing roles in both the exacerbation and the diagnosis of ADD.

171

Advertising "Causes" ADD by Training Us to Have a Short Attention Span

"There are two methods of fighting— the one by persuasion, the other by force; the first method is that of man, the second of beasts; but as the first method is often insufficient, one must have recourse to the second. It is therefore necessary for a prince to know well how to use both the beast and the man."
— Machiavelli, *The Prince*

Here's an odd coincidence:
In Russell A. Barkley's classic book *Attention Deficit Hyperactivity Disorder: A Handbook for Diagnosis and Treatment*, he points out several studies documenting that children with ADD (particularly those who also show signs of Conduct Disorder) are significantly more likely to smoke cigarettes.

In a recent article in *USA Today*, it was reported that RJR had found that rival brand Marlboro was successful in attracting new and young smokers because Marlboro advertising appealed to young men who were "rebels, risk takers, and those who liked sports and rock music." Wanting to go after this same market, RJR developed the Joe Camel ad campaign, rocketing that brand to the top of the sales charts with fierce brand loyalty among young adults, teenagers, and pre-teens. It's now estimated that 3000 children begin smoking every day in America, and that 1000 of them will eventually die of smoking-related diseases.

Could it be that advertising causes ADD? Or just that some savvy advertisers have identified ADD children and adults as an exploitable market? (Remember the "impulse buy" items that line the check-out areas of grocery stores?)

At first glance, the former seems absurd while the latter makes sense. And, in fact, impulsive people have long been considered the salesperson's dream, with seminars and sales trainings that have, for decades, stressed the importance of getting the customer to "buy now," whether the product is insurance or a new car.

But could it be possible that modern advertising practices do play a role in the explosion of ADD and ADD-like behaviors we see in the Western world?

Since the time of Aristotle, philosophers have pointed out that people are almost never static; it's not the nature of life to rest in one place or one state. Physics teaches this same concept in the notion of entropy—it's the nature of all things to decay into chaos unless continual energy is added to the system to prevent decay and collapse. Another example can be seen by observing the nature of an ADD teenager's bedroom when, for a week, his parent doesn't encourage him to clean it up.

The simple fact is that we're almost always either moving toward something or away from something. We're never stationary, static, held in one place, no matter how much that may seem to be the case.

Many people don't realize this (or that they can exert control over this, but that's another discussion, which you'll find in my book *Focus Your Energy*). Even fewer realize that their moving-toward or moving-away-from behavior is nearly always the result of a specific strategy to help them get what they want in life.

The Pain-Pleasure Continuum

The world of humans, we're told by psychologists such as Leif Roland, is made up of people who are either "moving toward pleasure, or moving away from pain." While everybody is theoretically capable of using either strategy, most people use one or the other as their primary way to stay motivated.

Those who use the "moving away from pain" strategy to keep themselves motivated visualize the terrible things that will happen to them if they fail to perform or reach their goals. When they begin to slack off at work, they think of the pain of being un-employed or yelled at by the boss, and that image pushes them from behind in a forward direction. Similarly, when they're presented with the possibility of poor social or personal choices (using drugs, having unprotected sex, skipping school, dropping out, driving too fast), they visualize the potential negative conse-quences of these behaviors. This pain-avoidance strategy causes them to decide to not engage in that behavior.

At the other end of the spectrum, people who use a "moving toward pleasure" strategy hold different mental images, feelings, or discussions with themselves to keep motivated. When they feel the urge to slack off at work, they visualize the raise they may get if they do an excellent job, or how good the praise from the boss will feel, or the warm glow of the recognition of their peers. They may even imagine the envy of others and hold to this picture: it's something to move toward. When times are tough for these folks, they look for the next thing, the new future, the golden oppor-tunity, using that light as a magnet to draw them forward.

Both of these strategies are useful, and both have their ap-propriate times and places. If we understand the primary motiva-tional strategy a person uses, then we can use that to keep them motivated. A "from pain" person will respond better to the threat of a failing grade, whereas a "toward pleasure" person will be more motivated by rewards.

Where this starts to break down, however, and where it may have to do with helping answer the question, "Why Do We Have ADD?" is when a person becomes stuck in one particular strategy and therefore loses access to the other.

A person stuck in the "from/avoid pain" strategy, for example, may become so obsessed with the idea of avoiding pain that they become completely averse to taking any sorts of risks. They avoid social situations because they fear making a fau paux, or avoid business confrontations for fear of bringing the wrath of the boss. They hesitate to make decisions (or agonize over them for mor-bidly long periods of time) because they're worried about the consequences of making the wrong decision.

On the other hand, a person stuck in the "move toward pleasure" strategy without access to an Avoid Pain strategy to balance them out may make wildly inappropriate decisions. They choose to take drugs because of the potential for a good feeling, for example, and fail to consider the consequences of the potential pain until they're already broke or in jail.

If we consider ADD to be composed primarily of the three behaviors of distractibility, impulsivity, and risk-taking, it would seem that folks with ADD are more solidly in the "Move Toward Pleasure" camp than in the Avoid Pain arena.

They're distractible because they're looking for the Next Pleasure. Much as a hungry person walking down the street will notice all the restaurants and bakeries, the pleasure-seeker is distracted by all the potential pleasure around him at the time. He may pursue these impulsively—without considering the potential pain they may cause—and thus make decisions which lead to the death of businesses, jobs, and relationships.

So, in this context, it's possible to redefine ADD as being a characteristic of those people who occupy the extreme end of the Pleasure-seeking spectrum, and hang out very rarely in the Pain-avoiding areas.

But if this is the case, where does this come from? Why do we have this type of ADD?

One possible explanation could be that modern children, particularly in the middle-and upper-middle class, where most ADD is diagnosed, are suffering from a surfeit of comfort. They rarely experience pain (hunger, deprivation, etc.) as did their grandparents who lived through the Great Depression. They haven't developed a strong sense of the need to avoid pain. Life has been easy; everything has essentially been handed to them on a silver platter. Another, even more insidious explanation is that our children are being conditioned to seek pleasure at the expense of learning how to avoid pain.

Three decades ago Vance Packard exposed the emerging marriage of psychology and advertising in his landmark book, *The Hidden Persuaders*. While some of Packard's claims bordered on the paranoiac (the naked women he saw in the ice cubes in the liquor companys' ads may have been more of his own personal Rorschach test than an intentional reality), nonetheless Packard did make an important and vivid contribution. Advertising in the

1950s and 1960s very much became a science, and that science was rooted in the notion of positive associative conditioning.

First, focus groups in an advertising company are held to determine what the strongest positive psychological images are that a person may respond to in relation to the product. Are women most attracted to a perfume's association with pastoral fields of wildflowers? Or are they most drawn to the muscled hunk who may hold them in his arms when he gets a whiff of their fragrance?

Thus an ad is created which continuously alternates between the most powerful known pleasurable image and the product.

The ideal result occurs when consumers walk into a store, notice a product on the shelf, and feel good when they see it. It's entirely irrational—or at least beyond the regions of rationality—and is experienced by most people at a level so visceral it's unconscious. They can't explain why they love a particular brand, but they just do.

Advertising and TV

Because the use of Approach Pleasure psychology is such a powerful strategy in advertising, the Avoid Pain strategy is rarely used. Instead of saying, "Use our deodorant so your armpits won't smell like the town dump," advertisers show images of attractive people of the opposite sex swooning when they get a whiff of the newly-aromatized pits.

For the average child or adult watching an average amount of television, each day brings—literally—thousands of these Seek Pleasure messages. Is it any wonder, then, that the MTV Generation's predominant motivational strategy is to seek pleasure? They've been taught that since before they could speak, watching cartoons and the Seek Pleasure commercials for everything from toys to breakfast cereals.

Another aspect of an individual's life strategies has to do with the notion of problem-solving. How do they react to stress? How do they evaluate and solve problems? With what depth can they see and analyze future situations and future problems, the consequences of their choices and their actions? Will they play checkers or chess—look for the quick fix or the five-moves-ahead strategy?

Again, here we see television as a powerful formative model.

On TV, virtually all of life's problems are solved in thirty to sixty minutes. On the rare occasion when that's not possible, the viewer can rest secure in the knowledge that the solution will come a week later, in the sequel. (Look at how frustrated and outraged many viewers become at sequels!)

If the first and most important message of television is always to seek pleasure and not bother with avoiding pain, then the second message is that all life's problems can be resolved quickly and easily. This, of course, reinforces the idea of the relative unimportance of avoiding pain: after all, why avoid something that will quickly be resolved in any case?

This additional theory of why we have so much ADD posits that the current explosion of ADD is traceable to the introduction of television. Modern psychologically-driven advertising methods penetrate the daily lives of people from birth through childhood and adolescence, and even into adulthood. Without the reality-check of something like the Great Depression or a World War, modern children are left assuming that life is about seeking pleasure at all times, and that avoiding pain is only a nuisance. Seek Pleasure becomes such a predominant part of their internal motivational landscape that they lose most of their ability to view a situation in terms of the pain it may cause. They don't realize that there are possible choices to minimize that pain.

This theory also offers an answer to the nagging question about the parents of today's ADD children, young adults and Baby Boomers. If ADD is genetic, and most ADD children have at least one similarly-afflicted parent, why was the parent able to finish school and keep a job, whereas the child is having trouble completing the seventh grade?

If we take this theory as one of the causative factors for why we have ADD, it would make sense that those children with the greatest tendency (genetically) toward ADD would be the most affected by the conditioning of TV and advertising. It doesn't mean ADD isn't genetic, nor does it mean that it's entirely caused by TV. But the combination is both powerful and often tragic.

Boomer parents, who weren't bombarded with the Seek Pleasure images to which their children were subjected, were able to develop at least functional Avoid Pain strategies to balance out their Seek Pleasure natural proclivities.

Solutions

There are two aspects to solving this problem: education and avoidance.

Education is the first and most important. I remember well the first time I was able to point out to one of my children lies in a TV advertising campaign, and how shocked she was to discover that everything said on TV wasn't the truth. Some people apparently haven't yet had this experience, and uncritically accept virtually everything advertisers shove at them, from foods to political candidates. It is possible, however, to teach our children how to critically examine an advertiser's claims, to find the self-serving distortions or misrepresentations of truth, and to accept or discard calls to action based on this knowledge.

With regard to avoidance, experts like Marie Winn and Vance Packard suggest that children should simply be kept away from large amounts of TV viewing, so their exposure to and conditioning from TV advertising is at a minimum. This will provide them with the self-assurance and independence of thought necessary to break through the impulse to seek pleasure uncritically whenever possible.

A Variation on Approach/Withdrawal: Why ADD Often Appears Different in Women than in Men

In men, we various ruling passions find,
In women, two almost divide the kind;
Those only fix'd, they first or last obey,
The love of pleasure, and the love of sway.
                                —Pope, *Epistle to a Lady*

Instead of viewing ADD as in relation to pleasure, many authorities would point to ADD as a problem of control over inhibition. The inhibitory mechanism of the brain (thought to reside in the right frontal lobe) isn't strong enough to stop or override impulses or desires. These are expressed whereas a person with better inhibition responses would have stopped himself. The ADD person blurts things out in conversation, indulges in impulsive sexual activity, spends money impulsively, and a host of similar activities commonly associated with ADD.

But there's an anomaly here. In her book *Women With ADD*, therapist Sari Solden points out that women with ADD are often "daydreamers," who drift through life paying only partial attention. They're usually not diagnosed as having ADD because the eruptive or externally impulsive behaviors so commonly identified with ADD are not showing.

I've also met women who are the "typical boy" type of ADD: outgoing, expressive, aggressive, and impulsive, and men who are the "typical girl" type of ADD—quiet and withdrawn, but constantly off in their own little dream world.

Assuming that in both cases what we're looking at really is ADD, then the approach/withdrawal continuum provides a ready answer for these two types of ADD. When a person is a born approacher, they'll exhibit their ADD in an external and expressive way. They'll lurch toward things they want, move from thing to thing, person to person, and have a life filled with wild variety and activity.

An avoider, however, will experience their ADD differently. Although they have the same lack of internal inhibition, they're prevented from expressing their impulsivity in the external world and in an external fashion. As a result, instead of interrupting others they interrupt themselves. Their daydreams and unwanted thoughts constantly interrupt their own stream of attention. They find that they can't pay attention in class, can't keep up with conversation, and are constantly losing things.

The reason we see the two types expressed largely through gender lines is because in our society men are mostly approachers and women are more likely to be avoiders. There's probably a solid genetic/evolutionary basis for this. Anthropologists and social scientists point out that the male imperative is to sow its genetic material as far and wide as possible, whereas the female imperative is to be cautious and careful on behalf of the young who are incapable of fending for themselves. While a man can theoretically impregnate hundreds of women in the course of a year, a woman can only become impregnated once. This leads to a natural tendency for men to be outer-directed approachers, and for women to be inner-directed avoiders.

That there are men who are avoiders and women who are approachers shows us the tremendous variety and adaptability of the human species, and may even, in itself, be some sort of ancestral/genetic adaptation.

In any case, it's one more possible glimpse of insight into why we have ADD, and why it has more than one face.

Solutions

Examining behavior and life's problems in the light of approach/withdrawal and the way these aspects of human nature affect us will often provide significant and useful insights into ways we can improve ourselves and our lives. It also gives us tools to change behavior, as much of approach and withdrawal behavior can be learned or brought under conscious control as we become more aware of it. This can also be excellent material to work with in psychotherapy.

We Lack Self-Discipline-Inducing Experiences in Childhood

In mans most dark extremity
Oft succor dawns from heaven.
— Sir Walter Scott, *The Lord of the Isles*

There are few humans on this earth for whom I have as much respect as I do for John Ratey, the psychiatrist and co-author of . For some time, John and I have carried on a lively email correspondence, and we recently did some all-day workshops together with Dr. Raun Melmed in Phoenix and Las Vegas. Often our discussions turn to the topic of why it is that some people with ADD, such as John, Raun, and myself, have been able to find what most people would call "success" in life, whereas others crash and burn, ending up in dead-end jobs, multiple marriages, or even in jail. What makes for the difference? Where did the "survivor" ability come from, or even the "success" ability?

Recently John sent me a short note over CompuServe, which became the basis for this section. He wrote: "Many of my patients who have had it very easy in their childhood do not do well in adult life. They just don't have the discipline—whether they have ADD or not—to respond to adversity. It seems that only if children fail or are tormented in their youth do they have the resilience to get back on the horse or pursue that to which they aspire as adults. I'm not talking just about a reactive response, that they're just trying to overcome barriers or win some prize somewhere. If the grace of Paul Tillich's God touches them, those who have faced adversity are set to respond, while the comfortable ones of the X generation are not so set to act and can't quite keep their brains in check."

My children now range in age from 14 to 22, and they've all heard stories about how their father had to walk four miles through the snow to get to and from junior high school. They never believed me, though; such a possibility was, to them, unthinkable, particularly in a modern city just 30 years ago.

Last Christmas when we visited my parents in Michigan I took them out in the car and clocked the distance from my parents' home to Walter French Junior High School and back. There was no bus for this route and I walked it every day, all school year, when I was 12, 13, and 14 years old. It was 3.6 miles round-trip. My kids were dumbfounded.

Psychologist and friend Michael Popkin mentioned over dinner recently how he'd heard the observation that business or financial success rarely moved down through more than three generations in families. "I sometimes wonder how much of a favor we're doing for our children by giving them such easy lives," he said. "It is not easy to deny them, though."

Billionaire Sam Walton, the late founder of WalMart and then-richest man in America, made the news just before his death a few years ago when his private life became public knowledge. He lived in a simple suburban house, drove an old mid-sized car, and gave his children only a small allowance of a few dollars a week. One must wonder if his children, and their children, will be better for having grown up in a thrifty middle-class environment, compared to, for example, the Kennedy clan which saw so many third-generation disasters.

Resilience, patience, and thrift are qualities that are learned not by lecture but by experience, and each requires that the experience be somewhat difficult or even painful. Yet these qualities are so often very lacking in the Boomer and X generations, sometimes leading to an "I don't care" attitude about schoolwork, relationships, and the workplace. The single most common complaint of business owners nationwide, according to dozens of studies over the past decade, is the difficulty in finding qualified, motivated, and loyal employees. The lack of loyalty to relationships is seen in the explosion of divorce nationwide (now becoming worldwide, as affluence and television travel around the globe), and the epidemic of unwed mothers and/or abortions.

Take as an example a child who seems unmotivated in school: He sporadically does his homework, and his teacher says he doesn't seem to care. His lack of motivation translates into easy boredom—after all, he doesn't care about the school work—which then looks like distractibility, impulsivity, and other characteristics of ADD. Soon he's carrying that as a label. While it may be true, it may also be that the deeper issue is the one driving his academic failure. An ADD person like Dr. Ratey was able to make it through medical school because the ADD was not as influential as core resiliences such as learning to persevere through adversity.

Solutions

This is a particularly tough issue: Parents instinctively want their children to have the best of everything. Yet by simply giving our kids things rather than forcing them to work for them, we send them the message that things have little value, that work is unnecessary, and, ultimately, that individual responsibility is meaningless.

Many thoughtful parents have responded to this by setting up work programs for their children within the home. The child does the laundry, or dishes, or mows the lawn, and, in return, gets a generous allowance to purchase clothing and other items. Now the clothes the child wears are a symbol of work, rather than of birthright. They got the very adult idea that everything we own we have to work for, one way or another. This is instilled before the child grows up, goes out in the world, and is hit in the face with that reality, so he's now prepared for it.

It may sound harsh or even radical, but in my humble opinion the parent who gives his child a car or a liberal allowance without commensurate work to earn it is doing that child more harm than good. The work ethic is a real and powerful thing, but it can only be learned by work.

Sunlight Starvation

"Good health! Whenever you go out of doors, draw the chin in, carry the crown of your head high, and fill the lungs to the utmost; drink in sunshine; greet your friends with a smile, and put soul into every hand-clasp.

—Elbert Hubbard

Back in the early decades of this century, most hospitals had solariums built into them—rooms where the walls and parts of the ceiling were made of glass and people could expose themselves to direct sunlight, often for hours at a time. This was not only accepted as generally healthy, but was considered a vital part of standard therapy for TB and a host of other then-incurable conditions.

The ancient Greeks used light as a therapy, as did the ancient Vedic physicians of India.

But from the late 1920's, when the first antibiotic drugs were coming into wide use, until the past decade, the use of light as a therapy was largely discarded. Recently, however, the importance of light has been rediscovered by scientists and physicians, largely as a result of research funded by the National Institutes of Mental Health.

We humans have spent ninety-nine percent of the past 300,000 years of our posited history on this earth in high-light environments, outdoors, chasing around the fields and plains and jungles for our food. In the past century—and particularly the past five decades—that's all changed. We now live in relatively dark caves we call houses, and work in dark caves we call offices or schools. Often the only time we're exposed to the outdoors is during the commute to and from work, and for many people in the northern half of the United States and across much of Europe that time is near-darkness, particularly during the winter months.

Because our eyes are so good at instantly adjusting to changes in the brightness of light around us, few people realize the radical difference in light between the office and outdoors. But consider these numbers: the average home or office is lit to a level of 200 to 300 lux (the theoretical equivalent of 200 to 300 simultaneous candles burning). A "brightly lit" office by modern architectural standards is 500 lux. But outdoors on a sunny day we're bathed by 50,000 to 100,000 lux, and even a dreary, cloudy, winter day will run from 5,000 to 20,000 lux.

The significance of this came out of these first NIMH studies, when it was discovered that one of the primary regulators of the amount of serotonin in the brain was the amount of light a person was exposed to. People with Seasonal Affective Disorder (SAD), a form of wintertime depression, had lower serotonin levels during the winter months. Their SAD went away, however, when they were exposed to several thousand lux of light every day through the use of "light boxes" that they would sit and look at. Other research has implicated light in levels of dopamine, another important neurotransmitter which has been implicated in ADD.

Studies performed at both the NIMH and in Germany have found that light deficiency can lead to many of the symptoms we've come to associate with ADD, such as distractibility, forgetfulness, and an apparent lack of motivation. These studies have been taken so seriously that the American Psychiatric Association is now including bright light therapy among its recommended arsenal of tools for psychiatrists, and many insurance companies will now pay for it.

While no one is suggesting that ADD is caused by a light deficiency, if the theories that ADD has to do with neurotransmitter-level abnormalities are true, then it may be that ADD could be made worse by our modern light-starved environment.

Several ADD individuals have reported to me how dramatically helped they were by daily jogging or walking. Most all attributed the improvement in their ADD symptoms to the exercise itself, yet one reported to me that when she started working out in a gym instead of jogging, she didn't get he same benefits. She assumed there was something unique for the body that had to do with a need for running, and there may be some truth to that, but if the NIMH studies are correct then a more likely answer is that jogging exposed her to high levels of light, whereas in the 500 lux gym she was still in a light-deprived environment.

So here is another of the many variables which may factor into why so many people have ADD or ADD-like symptoms, and particularly why there has been such an explosion of this over the past half-century: too little light.

Solutions

Get more sunlight.

Go outdoors on your lunch hour. Walk whenever possible, and spend time outside during the weekends. Put your desk near a window, and sit facing the window. Position your bed to an east-facing window, so you'll wake up to sunlight in the morning. If there's no east-facing window in your room, consider having a skylight or a Light Tunnel put in. Or get a timer and plug a 200 watt lamp into it, and set it for about 15 minutes before you want to wake up each morning. You'll discover that you're waking up more easily and effortlessly. (There are devices that you can order which will slowly build up to full brightness over a 15-30 minute period, simulating real dawn. They're listed in the book *Beyond Prozac*, by Michael Norden.)

We Lack Exercise

Better hunt in fields for health unbought,
Than fee the doctor for a nauseous draught,
The wise, for cure, on exercise depend,
God never made his work for man to mend.
— Dryden, *Epistles*

During the Kennedy administration a national program was instituted to get schoolchildren to exercise more. Physical education classes focused on aerobic and muscle-building exercise as much as on sports and skill-building, and during that decade children all across the country got a good workout daily during the school week.

Those were safer times, too, at least seemingly so. Children walked to school except in the most rural of areas, often traveling distances over a mile in each direction. This added to the exercise our children received. Today school busses populate the landscape nationwide and parents are loathe to let their children walk even a few blocks out of fear for their safety.

ADD experts Drs. Edward Hallowell and John Ratey, authors of *Driven To Distraction*, arguably the best book ever written on the subject of ADD, are outspoken about their belief in the value of exercise as a treatment for ADD. "Exercise is reliable, effective for most people, and has few side effects," John Ratey said at a recent conference in Phoenix. "I often recommend it be tried first before moving on to stronger therapies such as medication."

There's been a sixty percent decline from 1984 to 1994 in the number of high school students who get regular exercise. This startling statistic prompted Dr. Michael Norden to comment in his excellent book *Beyond Prozac*: "Once again we see modern life sharply diverging from ancestral life.... This lifestyle clearly contributes to today's serotonin deficiency."

As Dr. Norden points out, our ancestors got regular exercise by chasing or gathering their food. Today we're more likely to consider a request by the kids that we take them to the store—in the car—to be too much trouble.

And exercise doesn't just contribute to physical well-being. We know it causes an immediate and sustained increase in serotonin levels, as well. It oxygenates the brain which is, after all, only another organ of the body, and probably the one organ most dependent upon oxygen.

Numerous studies have shown how exercise improves mental acuity, reduces depression, and has an overall benefit on mood. Neuroscientist William Greenough of the University of Illinois found that rats which exercised in their youth had denser and more complex brains. He pointed out to *Newsweek* magazine in a recent article on children's brains that studies show that children who exercise regularly do better academically than their sedentary peers.

Similarly, University of Oregon education professor Robert Sylwester notes that children should not only exercise before, between, or after classes, but even during classes. In his book *A Celebration of Neurons* he points out that learning is most effective when it's multi-modal—involving tactile experience and motion as well as hearing and seeing.

So perhaps it could be that some of what looks like ADD is actually a reflection of the paucity of exercise we get.

Solutions

You don't need to join a club to get regular exercise. My wife and I have developed the habit of walking a few miles through the neighborhood every night after dinner; my parents walk the mall, and often log a few miles in an evening.

Some people like high-tech toys and buy exercise machines, but often get bored with them quickly. To solve this problem, one person told me that he put the machine in front of his TV set.

When he watches the morning news shows on TV and has his morning coffee, he's sitting on his exercise bicycle and pedaling for 20 minutes. It's a regular ritual, which keeps him at it, and it's not boring because of the distraction of the TV.

For children, exercise and outdoor activity is a necessity. Often this means that parents must ration TV, particularly during the daylight hours, and provide kids with incentives to join sports teams or participate in outdoor activities.

ADD is Useful in Our Workforce

Whatever may have been the case in years gone by, the true use for the imaginative faculty of modern times is to give ultimate vivification to facts, to science and to common lives, endowing them with the glows and glories and final illustriousness which belong to every real thing, and to real things only. Without that ultimate vivification—which the poet or other artist alone can give—reality would seem incomplete, and science, democracy, and life itself, finally in vain.
—Walt Whitman, *A Backward Glance O'er Traveled Roads*

A few years ago the *Wall Street Journal* ran an article on the front-page, left column, for which I've searched in vain ever since (I read it on a plane and left the paper behind). While I can't quote the article directly, the gist of it was that many corporate personnel people now look for a different personality profile in the people they're hiring from the criteria used in previous years.

Conventional wisdom for the past century has been that managers should look for the "slow and steady" person to fill a position in corporate America. People who had one job for a decade or more, and who left only because of a natural disaster or other unavoidable reason.

"Job hoppers"—those people who changed employers every year or two—were considered dangerous and to be avoided at all costs. After all, it can take half a year to get someone fully trained and up to speed, and there's considerable cost associated with that. When they just cut and run after a year or so it leaves a company high and dry, having to spend money to search for another employee and start the expensive training cycle all over again.

This article pointed out, however, that view is changing. While people who can't hold a job for over six months to a year are still considered a poor risk, someone who's changed jobs every two to four years is now, in many sectors, considered an asset.

According to this article such people bring with them to the job a breadth of knowledge about differing corporate cultures that is useful. They've picked up some strategies and insights at every job, seen a wider variety of things done right and wrong from which they could learn lessons than the average "slow and steady" person. These insights of theirs can contribute substantially to the corporate culture and company systems of an employer.

In this context, a touch of the wanderlust associated with ADD would be a good thing.

Similarly, children and adults who want to surf the Internet, or program and create Web pages in such a dynamic environment, must be highly creative and understand the needs of a short-attention-span medium. The entertainment environment in which our young people live is very fast-paced (complete with a TV show called "The Short Attention Span Theater"). It seems that the only part of their lives that still moves at 19th century speeds is school.

And even that is changing. With Chris Whittle's new Channel One educational TV channel coming into schools, and their increasing reliance on fast-paced media such as computers and video for instruction, being one of those "fast thinking" people may nowadays be as much an asset as a liability.

The first "revolution" was from hunting to farming, 12,000 years ago: the agricultural revolution. The second was about one hundred and fifty years ago—the industrial revolution, fueled primarily by the development of electric power grids in cities and the discovery of internal combustion engines which could exploit a cheap source of energy (oil). Both of these revolutions were well adapted to people with the Farmer mentality. They required linear-thinking skills and the ability to stand in one place for hours a day and put the same bolt on the same nut (or plant the same grain) time after time for years.

But in the past three decades, we've witnessed two more

revolutions. The first is the service industry revolution. A huge percentage of our workforce now are employed within the service sector—fast food, entertainment, advertising, marketing, cleaning—compared to just twenty years ago. In this sector, largely driven by salespeople, running at full speed is required. Kids diagnosed as ADD in school have a blast working at a fast food restaurant, and do very well in professions such as sales or marketing.

And the forth revolution—the big one—is the information revolution. More people are employed today in the United States in the business of providing or moving information than are employed in our factories. Fifty years ago, the only people in the information business were librarians, teachers, and writers, but now it's exploded across the country. One manifestation of this is the proliferation of online services such as CompuServe and the Internet, and there's even a new business category to go with them: "Information Providers." (This is a service I do in running the ADD Forum on CompuServe, for example. They consider me an IP or information provider.)

In the information age, speed is critically important. Information is accumulating and changing so rapidly that systems such as Telerate, Reuters, and others have adapted to transmit changes in the prices of currencies, for example, worldwide at nearly the speed of light. Fortunes are made and lost in moments, and decisions must be made and acted on with dazzling speed.

Consider how this change in technology and the speed of life is reflected in something as simple and basic as the home. How many contemporary families do you believe would—or even could—sit around the living room for two or three hours a night quietly reading? Or listening to the radio? While these were the norm one hundred, or fifty years ago, today's average family, both parents and children, would run out of the room screaming in boredom after an hour on the first night. Television producers well know how the attention span of Americans has changed over the past thirty years. The long-winded introductions of Ed Sullivan or skits of Ernie Kovaks have been replaced by shows where the shot never lasts more than seven seconds before the scene is cut to the next camera shot.

Newspapers reflect this change, too. Compare *USA Today* (an apt name in this context!) with any newspaper from the turn of the century.

So suddenly we're living in an environment uniquely well-adapted to the ADD individual. "I love to multitask," said Bill, a designer for an Atlanta ad agency. "With the computer, I can have three projects going at the same time, and when I get bored with one, I just hop to another." Work and channel-surfing are taking on an eerie resemblance to each other.

Cultural Anthropologist Cindy Smith is quoted in a recent issue of *Information Week* as saying that the clues to constructing a successful work environment in the Information Age are to be found among the hunter-gatherer tribes of the !Kung bushmen who live in Africa's Kalahari Desert. "The characteristics of virtual teams are high mobility, very weak notions of property – like having an office – and a high sense of egalitarianism," she says. "Exactly like the characteristics of a band of hunters and gatherers."

One of the largest computer companies in the world, Tandem Computers, Inc., is so impressed with her work that they've run the company as a "virtual workgroup" for over a decade. In just nine years, from 1991 to 2000, IW estimates that the number of people working from a "virtual office"- that is, working from home – will sextuple from 5 million to over 30 million. Between 1991 and 1995 the number doubled from 5 to 10 million.

So it shouldn't be surprising that this milieu has spawned a generation of short-attention-span individuals. They may, after all, be the ones best adapted to the brave new world we're entering, where the average individual has available to him with a laptop computer and modem an amount of information ten thousand times greater than the sum total of the knowledge and history of humanity just eighty years ago.

Solutions

Move in the direction of work, careers, and a lifestyle which uses and celebrates ADD, rather than trying to be a tax accountant, groaning under the daily weight of detail and calculations. And counsel the ADD child to do the same, even if their school is still stuck in the nineteenth century.

Our Lost Rituals

"With a good conscience our only sure reward, with history the final judge of our deeds, let us go forth to lead the land we love, asking His blessing and His help, but knowing that here on earth God's work must truly be our own."
—John F. Kennedy, Inaugural Address, 1/20/1961

In the late summer of 1995, I spent a week with Dr. Jane Shumway on an Apache Indian Reservation. We were doing in-service training for teachers and social workers, and spent most of our time with members of the tribe. We were invited to a number of sacred ceremonies, including a sweat and a puberty rite for a young girl.

This latter was fascinating. For four days, this girl and her family stood out in the desert. With the medicine men and friends and family supporting and encouraging her, she danced a religious dance to bring a blessing on her and to mark the transition from girl to woman.

Judy, one of the Apaches who hosted us, made a comment to me after we'd stood in the hot sun with this girl and her family dancing for six hours. "If she makes it through this, she'll know for the rest of her life that she's capable of anything."

Virtually every indigenous culture in the world has rites-of-passage rituals for its young, a reality that was not lost on Carl Jung, Margaret Mead, and other observers of human nature. It seems that ritual is a critical component to developing emotional and spiritual strength. Family rituals such as meals together, vacations, attending church or synagogue, etc., all serve to build the ties within a family and strengthen the members individually.

But in modern Western society, our historic and constructive rituals are breaking down. In their place, new rituals will necessarily emerge: it's a requirement of the human organism. And so we hear of gangs which require new members to rob or kill somebody, of fraternities who haze members to the point of death or injury, and roving gangs of suburban, middle-class teenagers who vandalize mailboxes, steal street signs, or compete to see how drunk they can become before they drive. These behaviors, as sick as they may seem, are actually fulfilling a basic human need for ritual and belonging.

But these rituals don't produce the kind of deep emotional strength that the family and larger-culture rituals of the past did. In many ways they're just hollow imitations, lacking in meaning and only transitory in their fulfillment of this inner need. This is similar to the way some people mistake sex for love, compulsively seeking it throughout their lives, never achieving satisfaction.

This loss of ritual may also address the deeper conundrum of modern-day ADD children: If ADD is genetic, then probably many of these children's parents are just as ADD as their kids. That being the case, how did those parents—themselves afflicted with ADD from birth—become sufficiently successful to end up in an upper-middle-class neighborhood? How did they get through school, college, relationships, and into the workplace?

One answer may be that they had rituals. Church and home were important in the pre-TV days. For the generation of my parents, the most common ritual of adulthood was to go off to war or participate in the war effort at home (WWII in their case). For their parents, there was the work involved in surviving the Great Depression or participating in World War One. Yet for my generation, going off to the Vietnam war was spectacularly unsatisfying and unnoble, and the protest riots were a poor substitute. Hippies and flower children sprang up as a community, context, and to provide ritual, but it was a largely dysfunctional culture for transition into "normal, American adult life." Our children have virtually no larger context for ritual, as families often no longer eat together (at least not without the TV), or worship together. Even the puberty transition ritual of graduating from high school has been minimized by the growing emphasis on a college education.

The Solution

How can we re-establish ritual for our children so they can grow up with the maturity and emotional stability which will allow them to succeed with or without ADD, as so many of their parents did?

Organizations exist which have historically provided this sort of ritual and context of belonging to children, although they are nowhere near as pervasive or important in American life as they were a generation ago. The Boy and Girl Scouts are probably the most well-known, but there are also others, many of them specific to particular religions. The Army, that rite of passage for my father, is still available but no longer mandatory. There are efforts in Congress to put into place public-service equivalents, commonplace in European countries such as Germany and Scandinavia where every teenager must serve in the military or in non-profit volunteer work after high school.

And, of course, working to strengthen family and local cultural rituals is an important step. Taking the kids to weekly worship, or to the symphony, or even to vacation together, builds that sense of shared experience and camaraderie that will become a strong foundation for later life.

ADD as a Challenge to Authoritarian Society

If a man does not keep pace with his companions, perhaps
it is because he hears a different drummer. Let him step to the
music which he hears, however measured or far away.
— Thoreau, *Walden*

Historically, whenever there has been social chaos, it's been accompanied by the rise of authoritarian leadership and institutions.

Hitler rose in Germany out of the ashes of that nation's defeat in World War I and the Great Depression. Mao Tze Tsung came to power in China after decades of weak government and the near-defeat of the Chinese by the Japanese war machine. Stalin responded to the uncertainty of the Russian people, and his message struck a responsive chord. As Iran stumbled back from the cultural upheavals and violent repression of the '60s under the CIA-installed and supported Shah, a demand for religious fundamentalism brought a theocratic government to power, as has happened in many other countries. Even here in the United States, we can see how times of uncertainty bring to the fore the shrill voices of those who would offer simple—and extreme—solutions to complex social, political, and economic problems.

So, too, the proliferation of the ADD diagnosis may reflect this trend on two levels: the search for simple answers to the complexities of human nature, and the desire of increasingly authoritarian institutions to modify "out of the norm" behavior.

Dr. Timothy Engelmann, who directs the Adult ADHD clinic

at Philhaven Behavioral Healthcare Services in Pennsylvania, recently emailed these observations to me:

"Part of the problem consists on a social-cultural level. Our society, as you point out in your Hunter's book, is becoming more rigidly rooted in the structuring of experience. Problems arise from rigid structuring. People vary in their ability to conform to this way of life, especially the ADHD person, who in repeated failures to respond to such structuring becomes labeled as 'disordered.'

"More disturbing, however, is that such structuring can be used as forms of social influence, which I believe limits the very nature of who we are as people."

Here we have in ADD a very complex set of behaviors and perceptions, encompassing a wide range of human experience. ADD is felt and expressed in dramatically different fashions from individual to individual.

Yet, like the call for flat taxes or balanced budgets or family values or organic food (all simplistic "solutions" to complex issues), the ADD diagnosis is viewed by many individuals and professionals as a sort of all-encompassing, cast-in-concrete certainty.

"People with ADD are more likely to..." is a phrase I've heard come from the mouths of dozens of professionals in the ADD industry, usually from a lectern. The sentence is finished with a wide variety of things, from "be in trouble with the law" to "have more car accidents" to "be promiscuous" to "fail in school." Rarely is it: "Be more creative," "be more interesting," "have more friends," "experience life in an uniquely rich way," or any other positive.

By having a nice, predictable box we can put people into, we seem to have resolved something. Labeling, in our society, often seems the same as fixing, but it's not, of course.

Dr. Englemann points out, "As social control becomes more pressing, the ADHD way of life actually becomes not only an asset, but an antidote to such limiting of experience."

But still, as society becomes more rigid, the search for nice little explain-all categories will continue and intensify. From the political arena, where a person can be dismissed with the wave of a hand and an, "Oh, he's a liberal," or "She's a conservative," to the social "I'm a Gen-X-er," to the technical "It's a Pentium machine," one-word labels seem to be the order of the day.

Similarly, as institutions come under attack from those who respond to the complex problems of society with simple answers, those institutions will become more rigid themselves, and therefore more prone to quick labeling and instant dismissal of individuals.

When "permissive" schools, for example, are attacked by politicians as the cause of a host of social ills, the schools will react by becoming less "permissive." They'll reactively categorize, label, and cram into consistent little slots as many children as they can. The end result will be (and is) an epidemic of diagnoses of ADD, oppositional-defiant disorder, etc.

As our institutions and culture become increasingly pressured and fractured, they'll respond by trying to find simple, one-word, quick-fix, easy-label answers. ADD is none of those, of course, but in the wrong hands it often has become exactly what the zealots would want.

Solutions

Beware the overfocused Farmers who want to set the rules and define the game.

Psychotherapist William J. Ronan of Minneapolis shared with me a year or so ago his "Farmer's Traits as a Disorder" paper:

The salient aspects of Farmers:

1. Unable to think tangentially. Tunnel vision. Miss subtle tangential environmental clues. Sees things as they have been told. Vigilant as in "vigilante."

2. Unable to remove nose from the grind stone, ending up with a smaller nose while having missed much of life's potential tangential inputs and experiences. Person is left singing, "Is That All There Is?"

3. Militaristic, rigid, inflexible, conservative. Possess no innate moral code. All morality is taught by and determined by external force. Does what s/he is told.

4. Loves monotony. Is able to take pride in marching in fours to the strains of a band.

5. *Process oriented: results are secondary. Believes in doing tasks the proper way, even if the "proper way" does not produce optimal results.*

6. *Can be easily led by illusionary goals. Believes in what they are told, regarding religious, political doctrine, repressed memories (false memory syndrome), etc., even when there is no objective support for the position. Calls gullibility and delusions "faith." Thinks of learning as memorization, and reasoning as "the devil's workshop."*

7. *Conformist, obedient to authority (see experiments performed by Stanley Milgram in 1963 when students were ordered to give shocks to other students). This is the group that Hitler aimed his political persuasion at in order to win his elections. Perfect choice for mob psychology.*

8. *Able to attend to small details while the larger picture is left unattended. May take pride in "getting the gas to Auschwitz on time," while either unwilling or unable to understand the larger implications. As a young male can easily be led to go halfway around the world and to kill people he doesn't know, for reasons he doesn't understand, philosophies he has never read, and economic theories of which nobody is certain. He will do this with extreme certainty because he was told to do so by "a person in authority."*

9. *Self-centered, within the context of group acceptance. Unable to take social risks. Will not say no to a social movement if it is perceived that this is what everybody else thinks. The Farmer is a person easily manipulated by society, and therefore valued by those elements in control of society.*

10. *Will easily adopt group ideology and abandon his/her own. Easily taken in by witch burning, McCarthyism, "Dittoheadism," and other similar social, political, and religious movements.*

SUMMARY:

What Is This Thing Called ADD, Anyway?

A DD has many different forms and faces, but all involve three basic components: distractibility, impulsivity, and risk-taking (or sensation-seeking). If you throw in restlessness and a high level of physical activity, you have ADHD or ADD-H, the "hyperactive" variation.

Scientists differ on what causes ADD. Seriously presented theories include the idea that it was useful at some time in the past (during the Hunting/Gathering phase of humanity). Other theories label it a psychological or psychiatric disorder, or it's also a wastebasket category that all too many different conditions are dumped into.

Scientists and physicians also argue about how ADD comes about in the brain. Is it a psychological disorder, caused by something in childhood or parenting (as hinted at by studies of identical twins where in 49% of cases only one of the twins had ADD/ADHD)? Or is it caused by heredity, the result of the brain being wired in a particular way that leaves a person distractible, impulsive, and a risk-taker (as the D4DR novelty-seeking gene studies indicate)? Or is it just part of the normal range of human behaviors, normally under control in people? Has it run out of control because of breakdowns in our homes, schools, society, and the impact of TV?

Nobody knows for sure.

What we do know is that there are a lot of people identified as having ADD, and that perhaps as many as a million are on some form of medication or treatment for the condition in the United States. The number of children and adults being diagnosed with ADD is skyrocketing, and, along with it, the sale of drugs like Ritalin. And following on the heels of that are the people who have an instinctive mistrust of the psychiatric profession. They are, in increasing numbers, claiming that the whole notion of ADD is just a "myth."

Whatever it is, it's definitely not a myth. ADD is real, and makes it difficult for children to succeed in normal public schools, and can be a curse to a person seeking a job as an accountant. On the other hand, ADD children in highly creative school environments often blossom, outperforming their non-ADD peers, and ADD adults seem particularly well-suited for fast-paced or high-risk occupations.

There are a variety of ways to deal with ADD, from taking medication to changing schools or jobs to learning new life skills (like how to get organized, or how to break big homework jobs into little chunks).

While my last book, *ADD Success Stories*, explored over a hundred specific strategies for being successful in school, relationships, and the workplace with ADD, this book has looked at the most fundamental question: *What is ADD, anyway, and why is there so much of it?* Having read this far, you're probably close to sharing my belief on the topic: it isn't as simple as most people claim, and the solutions may well be found in understanding the causes. And the causes, clearly, are not always the same for every person.

Hopefully this book has provided some nourishing food for thought. Others will take some of the themes and ideas explored here and put them to a more scientific evaluation. But for now we'll have to content ourselves with the certainty that we don't know for sure what ADD is, where it came from, or even how to most effectively treat it. There is honest and understandable disagreement among even the most well-informed researchers in the field, and this is unlikely to resolve itself anytime soon.

As we all go forward in our personal or professional searches for the answers, however, I send this final greeting: happy hunting!

Chapter Notes

Chapter One: ADD is Profitable for Business

Paul J. Gerber, Rick Ginsberg, and Henry B. Reiff, "Identifying Alterable Patterns in Employment Success for Highly Successful Adults with Learning Disabilities" (pp475-487), The Jounal of Learning Disabilities, Volumne 25, Number 8, October 1992.

Stephen J. Wolin and Sybil Wolin, *The Resilient Self: How Survivors of Troubled Families Rise Above Adversity,* Villard Books, Random, 1993.

Chapter Two: Education and Our Children

Newsweek, November 13, 1989.

Forbes, November 21, 1994.

James T. Webb and Diane Latimer, *ERIC Digest* #522, "ADHD and Children Who Are Gifted."

"The Effects of Medication and Curriculum Management on Task-Related Behaviors of Attention Deficit Disordered and Low Achieving Peers," V.P. Thompson, E.E. Gickling, J.F. Havertape, Monograph on Behavorial Disorders, Council for Exceptional Children. 1983 86-87.

Marie Winn, The Plug-In Drug.

Bruno Bettelheim, *The Uses of Enchantment.*

Chapter Three: Genetics and Psychology

John Hallowell and Edward Ratey, *Driven to Distraction,*Simon & Schuster, 1994.

Time magazine, *March 24, 1995.*

Discover magazine, February, 1994.

Jay Fikes, Ph.D.

Jacob Bronowski, *The Ascent of Man*, Little Brown, 1973.

Craig Stanford, *Chicago Tribune*, reprinted 5/1/95 in the *Atlanta Constitution*.

Claudio Naranjo, "On The Psychology of Meditation," 1971.

Shunryu Suzuki, *Zen Mind, Beginner's Mind*, Weatherhill, New York & Tokyo, 1970.

Rabbi Isaac Luria, *Ten Luminous Emanations*.

Abraham Maslow, *Motivation and Personality*, Harper & Row, 1954.

Ugo Betti, *The Inquiry*, 1944.

Rabindranath Tagore, *Stray Birds*, 1976.

"The Paradoxical Effect." In recent years even the term "paradoxical effect" has been discarded although there is still no clear, scientific explanation for how or why stimulant drugs work to calm down hyperactive kids.

"A twin study of hyperactivity: II. the aetiologyical role or genes, family relationships, and perinatal adversity." *Journal of Child Psychology and Psychiatry*, 30, 691-709.

Edward Hoffman, interview Abraham Maslow (1968), *Psychology Today*, (pp 68) January-February 1992.

Chapter Four: Social Adaptations

Wilson Harrell, *For Entrepreneurs Only*, Career Press, 1994.

Dr. Rupert Sheldrake, *The Presence of the Past*, Park Street Press, 1988.

Dr. Marc Lappé, *Evolutionary Medicine: Rethinking the Origins of Disease*, page 41, Sierra Club Books, San Francisco, 1994.

Chapter Five: The Stress and Toxicity of Modern Life

Connirae Andreas and Tamara Andreas, *Core Transformation: Reaching the Wellspring Within*, Real People, 1994.

K.A. Miczek (ed), *Ethopharmacology: Primate Models of Neuropsychiatric Disorders*, New York: Liss.

Michael J. Norden, *Beyond Prozac*, Regan Books, New York, 1995.

Mike Feinsulber, "National Glumness Explained," Associated Press, November 26, 1995.

National Sleep Foundation, "America Getting Sleepier," Associated Press, December 6 1995.

Sandra Arbetter M.S.W., *Current Health Magazine*, "Violence: A Growing Threat," (pp 6-12), February 1995.

Chapter Six: Brain Chemistry and Physiology

Textbook of Clinical Chiropractic, Williams & Wilkins, Baltimore, 1993.

One, published in 1989 by chiropractors JM Giesen, DB Center, and RA Leach in the *Journal of Manipulative Physiological Therapy* (12:353-363).

Nancy L. Girardi, et al., "Blunted catecholamine responses after glucose ingestion in children with attention deficit disorder," *Pediatric Research*, 38(4):539-542, 1995. For reprints, write to William V. Tamborlane, MD, Department of Pediatrics, Yale School of Medicine, 333 Cedar St., New Haven, CT 06510.

In an interview in the Winter, 1996 edition of *Attention!* magazine (the publication of C H.A.D.D.), Dr. Judith Rapoport, in *Attention!* magazine.

Dr. Ruben C. Gur, director of brain behavior laboratory at the University of Pennsylvania studies gender differences. *Associated Press*, January 26, 1995.

Broda Barnes, M.D., *Hypothyroidism: The Unsuspected Illness*, Harper & Row, New York, 1976.

Chapter Seven: Contemporary Lifestyles and Habits

Russell A. Barkley, *Attention Deficit Hyperactivity Disorder: A Handbook for Diagnosis and Treatment*, Guilford Press, 1990.

USA Today, November 16th, 1995.

Sari Solden, *Women With Attention Deficit Disorder*, Underwood Books, Grass Valley, CA, 1995.

Newsweek, May 19, 1996.

Information Week, Cindy Smith quote, 1/22/96.

About the Author

Thom Hartmann first encountered ADD when he worked as the executive director of a residential treatment facility for abused and abandoned children in New Hampshire. During his five years as Executive Director of the New England Salem Children's Village, it grew into one of the most highly respected facilities in the state. Thom co-founded the New Hampshire Group Home Association, and worked closely with that state's governor to create programs for children and adults in crisis.

Out of that experience, and the ADD diagnosis of one of his own children, he wrote his first book on the subject of ADD, *Attention Deficit Disorder: A Different Perception* (Underwood Books, 1993). It is currently one of the best-selling books in the field and was the subject of an article in *Time* magazine. Combining his business experience with his knowledge of ADD, he followed this with a second book, *Focus Your Energy: Hunting For Success in Business with Attention Deficit Disorder* (Pocket Books, 1994).

In *ADD Success Stories*, Hartmann assembled a collection of specific strategies and techniques which children and adults with ADD can use to be more successful in life. These strategies are illustrated with scores of first-person stories.

Think Fast! The ADD Experience!, edited with Janie Bowman, collects dialogues, experiences and advice on ADD from worldwide on-line sources.

An international entrepreneur, the author of over 200 published articles, and an on-site negotiator in third-world countries for the international Salem relief organization, Hartmann also runs the Attention Deficit Disorder Forum on CompuServe, where he can be reached at 76702,765.

Index

A

adaptive, 60
ADD and Trout, 73
addiction, 87-89, 91
addictive, 87
Admiral Perry, 98
adrenaline, 56, 76, 78, 134
adventure, 77
agoraphobia, 85
Agricultural Age, 119
agricultural revolution, 54, 57,
   60-61, 193
agriculture, 58, 60
alcohol, 9, 86-88, 124, 131, 144
Aldine's First Language Book,
   26-27
amphetamine, 77, 130
anthropological basis of ADD, 59
Antichrist, 140
anxiety, 134, 136
Armageddon, 140
artificial colors, 152
ascertainment bias, 13
aspirin, 149, 152
attention span of Americans, 194
authoritarian leadership and institutions, 199

B

B-2 bomber, 33
Benzedrine, 131
Bonhoeffer, Dietrich, 21

biofeedback, 62
biological stasis, 70, 75, 77
bipolar disorder, 126-127
Bodhisattva vow, 70
Bradford, Beth, 150-151
bright children, 29-32
Bronowski, Jacob, 60
Buddhist thought, 70

C

caffeine, 77, 124, 132
cancer diagnosis, 3
caste system, 57
catecholamine responses, 154
Cayce, Edgar, 138
cerebral cortex, 66
Challenge Model, 8
channel-surfing, 195
chiropractors, 150-151
chromium, 127
Chronic Fatigue Syndrome,
   (CFS), xiv, 10
CIBA, 5
cingulate gyrus, 160
Civilization and Its Discontents, 108
cocaine, 77, 130
coffee, 87, 131-132, 167-168
cognitive processes, 75
Collapse of the Middle Class, 134
compulsion, 87-88, 91
compulsive, 87
compulsive gambler, 77

compulsive talking, 87
CompuServe, 12, 14, 32, 117,
    130, 183, 194
copper, 127
cortex, 66-69, 74, 78, 80
crisis, 78
critical thinking skills, 21
cultures, 58, 62

D

D4DR, 203
D4DR gene, 165
death wish, 73
deBronkart, Dave, 117
depression, 126-127, 130, 134
Dexedrine, 130-131, 163
Diagnostic and Statistical Man-
    ual of Mental Disorders, 7
diet pills, 131
disability, 107
discrimination, 13
diseases of domesticated ani-
    mals, 58
disorder, 107
distractibility, 54-55, 63, 74-75,
    79, 85, 92
dopamine, 165, 187
dopamine receptors, 165
Dr. Bradley, 131
Driven To Distraction, 183, 189
drug abuse, 127
drugs, 87
DSM (Diagnostic and Statisti-
    cal Manual of Mental Disor-
    ders), 7
Dylan, Bob, 140

E

Eddington, Sir Arthur, 101
EEG Neurofeedback, 5, 111, 158
encephalitis, xv
end-of-the-world, 141
endocrine system, 167-168
Engelmann, Timothy, 199
entrepreneur, 77
epinephrine, 154
Evolutionary Medicine, 107
exercise, 87

F

factory farming, 168
family rituals, 196
famines, 141
Farmer's Traits as a Disorder,
    201
Feingold, Ben, 149-152
Fichte, 18-19
fight or flight, 84, 87
fight-or-flight response, 67
Freud, Sigmund, 63, 70, 72-73,
    108, 130
frontal lobes, 75, 78
fruits, 128

G

gambling, 87
Gestalt therapy, 89, 92
Gide, Andre, 77
gifted children, 15, 28-33
Gingko, 132
glucose, 154
Grooms, Gary, 89

H

Hallowell, Edward, 56, 84, 163, 189
Hammerschmidt, Dale, 12
harm avoidance, 165
Harrison's Principles of Internal Medicine, 134
heart attacks, 152
hierarchy of needs, 70
Hinduism, 62, 70
home schooling, 33, 43
homeless, 133
Homeschooling, 23
Hong Kong, 17
hopping from job to job, 85
Humanistic Psychology, 51, 71
Hundredth Monkey Phenomenon, 101, 105
hunting gene, 57
hypoglycemia, 154
Hypothyroidism, 167–168

I

Id, 72
identical twins, 81
impatience, 55
impulsive, 203
impulsivity, 53, 55, 74–76, 79, 85, 92
India, 57, 61-62
Industrial Age, 119
industrial revolution, 193
industrial society, 57
Information Age, 110, 118–119
information revolution, 194

insulin, 154
internal motivational landscape, 178
Internet, 193–194
iodine, 168
iron, 127

J

Japan, 17, 57, 63
Japanese society, 98
Jesus, 70
job hoppers, 192

K

!Kung bushmen, 195
Kabbalah, 70
Kennedy, John F., 77, 115
Kolberg, Judith, 112, 114

L

L-tryptophan, 127
labeling, 200–201
Laplanders, 60
lead poisoning, 123
Learning Disabilities, 164
Learning Skills, 26-27
Life Wish, 73
light as a therapy, 186
limbic system, 160, 164
Lithium, 126-127
Luria, Rabbi Isaac, 70
Lynn, George, 79, 91, 93

M

manganese, 127
mania, 126
manic-depressive, 126
Marley, Bob, 140
Maslow, Abraham, 51, 65, 67, 70-71, 78-79, 81-83
masturbation, 87
meditation, 111
Melmed, Raun, 183
mental illness, 8-9, 12-13
minerals, 126-128, 136
Minimal Brain Damage (MBD), xv
Minimal Brain Dysfunction, xv
misfits of British society, 99
molasses, 127
Morphic Resonance, 101, 104-105
Morphogenic Field, 105
music, 68-69, 73, 91

N

Napoleon, 15, 18
National Institutes of Mental Health (NIMH), 53, 110
need to experience aliveness, 71-72, 75, 78, 83
need to reduce uncertainty, 97
Nesse, Randolph, 56
Neuro Linguistic Programming, (NLP) 92
neurochemicals, 87
neurochemistry, 65, 81, 84, 130
nicotine, 124, 131

noradrenaline, 134, 144
norepinephrine, 154
Nostradamus, 139-140
novelty seeking, 165
Nuclear Magnetic Resonance (NMR), 156
nuclear meltdowns, 141
NutraSweet, 153-154

O

old souls, 141-142
open-faucet-thalamus, 69
overcommitment, 78
ozone layer, 141

P

Paradoxical Effect, 77
Pascal, 72
Pavlov, 101-102
PCB, 124
Pediatric Research, 154
persistence, 165
PET scans, 156, 159
polychlorinated biphenyl (PCB), 123
Popkin, Michael, 184
Post Traumatic Stress Disorder (PTSD), xiv
pre-TV days, 197
procrastination, 78
promiscuity, 87
Prostatic Specific Antigen (PSA), 3
Prozac, 88, 130
Prussia, 15, 18-20, 22

psychologically-driven advertising, 178
Psychology Today, 81-82

R

radioactive dyes, 156
rage, 79
Ratey, John, 56, 75, 84, 163, 183, 185, 189
Reagan, Ronald Wilson, 139
Real Schulen, 20
religious rituals, 62-63
remote shared learning, 103
René Descartes, 71
research, 13
Reticular Activating System (RAS), 67-69, 71-72, 74, 76-77, 79-80
reward dependence, 165
risk, 77
risk-taking/restlessness, 53
Ritalin, 5, 22, 32, 77, 129-130, 132, 163, 167-168, 204
rites-of-passage rituals, 196
rituals, 197-198
Roland, Leif, 38-39, 174
Ronan, William J., 201

S

salicylates, 149, 152
scanning, 54, 59-60, 74, 85
school culture, 25
Seasonal Affective Disorder (SAD), 187
seizures, 127
self-actualization, 70, 79, 82

Selye, Hans, 134
Serotonin, 126-127, 144, 187, 190
service industry revolution, 194
sex, 73, 77, 82, 86-87, 113, 175, 197
Shao Lin martial arts, 89
Sheldrake, Rupert, 101, 104-105
shopping, 87
social control, 200
SPECT scans, 156
speed rap, 129
spicy foods, 73
SSRI (Selective Serotonin Re-uptake Inhibitors), 88, 91
Stewart, Al, 140
stimulant drugs, 51, 77
stress, 133-137, 141
stress responses, 84
strokes, 152
subluxations, 150
success, 60
sugar, 153-155
sugar cane, 127
suicide, 127, 131, 139, 143-144
Sweden, 17

T

Tagore, Rabindranath, 71-72
Taiwan, 17-18, 23
talented children, 21, 28, 30
television, 171, 177-178, 185, 194
Ten Luminous Emanations, 70
thalamic gain, 51, 84

thalamic, 77

thalamus, 66-69, 71-72, 74, 76-77, 79-80, 164

The Journal of Orthomolecular Psychiatry, 150

The Perception of Time, 116-117

Thorazine, 35-36

thyroid, 167-169

thyroid gland, 167

tobacco, 87, 131

toxic-waste spills, 141

U

Unabomber, 108

Underwood, Tim, 135

unthinkable behaviors, 75

upper-middle-class neighborhoods, 35

upper-middle-class white neighborhoods, 35

US Commissioners of Education, 20

V

vegetables, 128

virtual office, 195

vitamin B6, 127

vitamin C, 126

vitamin E, 126-127

vitamins, 127-128

vivid colors, 73

Volksschule, 19-20

W

Waldron, Lamar, 30

Weiss, Lynn, xiv

Williams, George, 56

Wilson Harrell, 99-100, 118

Wolin, Stephen, 8

Wolin, Sybil, 8

Z

Zen, 63

zinc, 127

Attention
Deficit
Disorder

A Different Perception

Thom Hartmann

Foreword by Michael Popkin, Ph.D.

Thom Hartmann sees ADD sufferers as "hunters" — totally focused on movement, constantly monitoring their environment, exhibiting incredible bursts of energy. These "hunters" find themselves in a contemporary society of "farmers" (cautious, slow and steady workers).

As many as 20 million Americans may suffer from ADD. This is the first book to explain that ADD may be beneficial. It identifies ADD individuals who changed the world, like Ernest Hemingway, Thomas Edison, and Benjamin Franklin. Hartmann, the father of an ADD child, explains how adults and children with ADD can adapt and function more creatively and productively. His remarkable "hunters in a farmer's world" theory was profiled in *Time* magazine.

$10.95, Trade paper, 162pp, ISBN 1-88733-156-4

Available at bookstores everywhere or call (800) 233-9273 to order
Bulk discounts for ADD groups are available at (800) 788-3123